MACMILLAN MASTER GUIDES

£2.50

CW00418052

GENERAL EDITOR: JAMES GIB...

JANE AUSTEN	*Emma* N...
	Sense and ...
	Persuasio...
	Pride and ... ...son
	Mansfield Park Richard Wirdnam
SAMUEL BECKETT	*Waiting for Godot* Jennifer Birkett
WILLIAM BLAKE	*Songs of Innocence and Songs of Experience* Alan Tomlinson
ROBERT BOLT	*A Man for All Seasons* Leonard Smith
CHARLOTTE BRONTË	*Jane Eyre* Robert Miles
EMILY BRONTË	*Wuthering Heights* Hilda D. Spear
JOHN BUNYAN	*The Pilgrim's Progress* Beatrice Batson
GEOFFREY CHAUCER	*The Miller's Tale* Michael Alexander
	The Pardoner's Tale Geoffrey Lester
	The Wife of Bath's Tale Nicholas Marsh
	The Knight's Tale Anne Samson
	The Prologue to the Canterbury Tales Nigel Thomas and Richard Swan
JOSEPH CONRAD	*The Secret Agent* Andrew Mayne
CHARLES DICKENS	*Bleak House* Dennis Butts
	Great Expectations Dennis Butts
	Hard Times Norman Page
GEORGE ELIOT	*Middlemarch* Graham Handley
	Silas Marner Graham Handley
	The Mill on the Floss Helen Wheeler
T. S. ELIOT	*Murder in the Cathedral* Paul Lapworth
	Selected Poems Andrew Swarbrick
HENRY FIELDING	*Joseph Andrews* Trevor Johnson
E. M. FORSTER	*A Passage to India* Hilda D. Spear
	Howards End Ian Milligan
WILLIAM GOLDING	*The Spire* Rosemary Sumner
	Lord of the Flies Raymond Wilson
OLIVER GOLDSMITH	*She Stoops to Conquer* Paul Ranger
THOMAS HARDY	*The Mayor of Casterbridge* Ray Evans
	Tess of the d'Urbervilles James Gibson
	Far from the Madding Crowd Colin Temblett-Wood
BEN JONSON	*Volpone* Michael Stout
JOHN KEATS	*Selected Poems* John Garrett
RUDYARD KIPLING	*Kim* Leonée Ormond
PHILIP LARKIN	*The Whitsun Weddings* and *The Less Deceived* Andrew Swarbrick

MACMILLAN MASTER GUIDES

D.H. LAWRENCE	*Sons and Lovers* R. P. Draper
HARPER LEE	*To Kill a Mockingbird* Jean Armstrong
LAURIE LEE	*Cider with Rosie* Brian Tarbitt
GERARD MANLEY HOPKINS	*Selected Poems* R. J. C. Watt
CHRISTOPHER MARLOWE	*Doctor Faustus* David A. Male
THE METAPHYSICAL POETS	Joan van Emden
THOMAS MIDDLETON and WILLIAM ROWLEY	*The Changeling* Tony Bromham
ARTHUR MILLER	*The Crucible* Leonard Smith *Death of a Salesman* Peter Spalding
GEORGE ORWELL	*Animal Farm* Jean Armstrong
WILLIAM SHAKESPEARE	*Richard II* Charles Barber *Othello* Tony Bromham *Hamlet* Jean Brooks *King Lear* Francis Casey *Henry V* Peter Davison *The Winter's Tale* Diana Devlin *Julius Caesar* David Elloway *Macbeth* David Elloway *The Merchant of Venice* A. M. Kinghorn *Measure for Measure* Mark Lilly *Henry IV Part I* Helen Morris *Romeo and Juliet* Helen Morris *A Midsummer Night's Dream* Kenneth Pickering *The Tempest* Kenneth Pickering *Coriolanus* Gordon Williams *Antony and Cleopatra* Martin Wine *Twelfth Night* R. P. Draper
GEORGE BERNARD SHAW	*St Joan* Leonée Ormond
RICHARD SHERIDAN	*The School for Scandal* Paul Ranger *The Rivals* Jeremy Rowe
ALFRED TENNYSON	*In Memoriam* Richard Gill
EDWARD THOMAS	*Selected Poems* Gerald Roberts
ANTHONY TROLLOPE	*Barchester Towers* K. M. Newton
JOHN WEBSTER	*The White Devil* and *The Duchess of Malfi* David A. Male
VIRGINIA WOOLF	*To the Lighthouse* John Mepham *Mrs Dalloway* Julian Pattison
WILLIAM WORDSWORTH	*The Prelude Books I and II* Helen Wheeler

MACMILLAN MASTER GUIDES

TO THE LIGHTHOUSE

BY VIRGINIA WOOLF

JOHN MEPHAM

MACMILLAN

First published 1987 by
MACMILLAN PRESS LTD
Houndmills, Basingstoke, Hampshire RG21 2XS
and London
Companies and representatives
throughout the world

ISBN 0–333–43277–0

A catalogue record for this book is available
from the British Library.

11 10   9   8   7   6   5   4   3   2
03   02   01   00 99 98 97 96 95 94

Printed in Malaysia

CONTENTS

GENERAL EDITOR'S PREFACE

The aim of the Macmillan Master Guides is to help you to appreciate the book you are studying by providing information about it and by suggesting ways of reading and thinking about it which will lead to a fuller understanding. The section on the writer's life and background has been designed to illustrate those aspects of the writer's life which have influenced the work, and to place it in its personal and literary context. The summaries and critical commentary are of special importance in that each brief summary of the action is followed by an examination of the significant critical points. The space which might have been given to repetitive explanatory notes has been devoted to a detailed analysis of the kind of passage which might confront you in an examination. Literary criticism is concerned with both the broader aspects of the work being studied and with its detail. The ideas which meet us in reading a great work of literature, and their relevance to us today, are an essential part of our study, and our Guides look at the thought of their subject in some detail. But just as essential is the craft with which the writer has constructed his work of art, and this may be considered under several technical headings – characterisation, language, style and stagecraft, for example.

The authors of these Guides are all teachers and writers of wide experience, and they have chosen to write about books they admire and know well in the belief that they can communicate their admiration to you. But you yourself must read and know intimately the book you are studying. No one can do that for you. You should see this book as a lamp-post. Use it to shed light, not to lean against. If you know your text and know what it is saying about life, and how it says it, then you will enjoy it, and there is no better way of passing an examination in literature.

JAMES GIBSON

ACKNOWLEDGEMENTS

The author and publishers wish to thank the following who have kindly given permission for the use of copyright material: The Hogarth Press Ltd and the Estate of Virginia Woolf for extracts from *To the Lighthouse* by Virginia Woolf.

The edition of *To the Lighthouse* to which I have given page references in brackets after quotations in this book is the paperback edition published by Granada (London, 1977).

Cover illustration: *Green Jug and Brush Pot* by Duncan Grant. Photograph © private collection, reproduced by courtesy of the Anthony d'Offay Gallery.

1 VIRGINIA WOOLF: LIFE AND BACKGROUND

Virginia Stephen was born in 1882. Her father, Leslie Stephen, was a well-known intellectual, and he was fifty years old when Virginia was born. As a young man he had made a name for himself as a mountaineer, and he later become a very hard-working, professional man of letters; he was an essayist, magazine editor, biographer, philosopher and historian of ideas. His most celebrated work was the monumental 65 volume *Dictionary of National Biography*, of which he was the editor for many years as well as the main contributor. He lived with his very large household in a rather crowded house near Hyde Park in London. He was always worried about money, about how to support the extensive establishment that he accumulated. This consisted, during Virginia's childhood, of her parents, her sister and two brothers, three children from her mother's first marriage and one (a mentally handicapped girl) from her father's previous marriage, plus of course numerous servants, visitors and guests.

Virginia's mother, Julia Stephen, was a much admired woman, whose first husband, whom she greatly loved, had died young. When Leslie Stephen proposed to her she was a sad young widow, beautiful, severe, deeply committed to charity work among the poor and sick. She took upon herself the considerable job of running the ever-expanding Stephen household and bearing the Stephen children. In spite of these burdens she continued also with her charity work which was no mere hobby for her. As a Victorian middle class mother, she could not obtain the professional training and status that might have been open to her in a later age. She pursued her work as a nurse and as what we would now call a social worker and wrote a pamphlet 'On the Management of the Sick Room'. She was an extremely busy woman and it is possible that exhaustion contributed to her sudden death in 1895.

Leslie and Julia Stephen are the models for Mr and Mrs Ramsay in *To the Lighthouse*. The family went every year to St Ives in Cornwall and it was Virginia's memories of these long and happy holidays that are the basis for the family scenes in Part I of the novel, where they have been transferred to an island in Scotland. She was haunted by the memory of her parents until 1925 when, at the age of 43, she wrote *To the Lighthouse*. It is worth stressing that when Virginia Stephen was seven (Cam's age in Part 1 of *To the Lighthouse*), her father was approaching 60 years of age and that her mother died when she was still only thirteen years old.

The Stephen family was shattered by a series of deaths. Virginia's adored step-sister Stella died soon after marrying in 1897, her father died after a long illness in 1904 and her older brother Thoby died of a fever contracted while travelling in Greece in 1906. Virginia was distressed to the point of mental instability by these traumatic events. She suffered periods of severe mental ill-health and she attempted suicide on several occasions. All her life she remained vulnerable to the return of devastating emotions (as does Lily Briscoe in *To the Lighthouse*) and to anxiety and uncertainty about her life and her work. She herself appears in the novel in fragmented parts as both Cam, a child and later an adolescent who struggles to work out her relationship with her father, and as the artist Lily Briscoe who mourns Mrs Ramsay and attempts to celebrate her in her work.

After the death of their father the Stephen sisters moved away from Kensington, which they found to be an oppressive, snobbish, Victorian milieu. They set up house in the Bloomsbury district of London and there formed around them a group of friends, mostly young men from Cambridge University, who thought of themselves as representing progressive, modern culture. This circle of friends instituted for themselves a relaxed, liberated regime of sexual and social manners and they became known as the Bloomsbury Group. This included Lytton Strachey, a writer who modernised the art of biography; Roger Fry, an art critic who shocked England with two exhibitions of Post-Impressionist art in 1910 and 1912; John Maynard Keynes, who revolutionised economics and James Strachey who translated the works of Sigmund Freud. Other authors, among them E.M. Forster and T.S. Eliot, also became loosely associated with the Bloomsbury Group and friends of Virginia Woolf. Virginia's sister Vanessa became a well-known painter in a subdued post-impressionist style and married a celebrated writer, Clive Bell.

Vanessa Bell managed to combine her successful career as a painter with a fruitful domestic life, having three children and a series of lovers, in striking contrast with the painter Lily Briscoe in *To the Lighthouse*.

In 1913 Virginia Stephen married Leonard Woolf, another of her brother's friends from Cambridge. He became a professional editor and writer. His main interest was in politics. He wrote for the influential magazine *The New Statesman* and was very active in the Labour Party. He was an important figure in the campaigns for the foundation of the League of Nations and later for the independence of India. Together Leonard and Virginia Woolf founded the Hogarth Press which became a successful publishing house. They had no children as they had been told that it would be inadvisable because of Virginia's uncertain health. Often in her life Virginia Woolf seems to have regretted this lack of children and to have wondered whether her career as a writer would have been impossible to combine with having children.

This circle of creative, modern thinkers and writers was the immediate context for Virginia's Woolf's work. More broadly, she read and was deeply influenced by Proust. She read and was intrigued by James Joyce's *Ulysses* when it was published in 1919. She also encountered the modern technique of 'stream of consciousness' narration in the many-volumed novel *Pilgrimage* by Dorothy Richardson. The author with whom she felt most affinity was the New Zealand writer Katherine Mansfield.

Virginia Woolf's early novels *The Voyage Out* (1915) and *Night and Day* (1919) were modestly successful and were traditional in style. It was with her next novels, *Jacob's Room* (1922) and *Mrs Dalloway* (1925) that she began the experiments with narrative technique that were to establish her as a leading literary modernist and to develop her individual style of lyrical, poetic fiction. She started to write *To the Lighthouse* in 1925 and it was published in 1927. It was a success and introduced her to a wider readership and she was from this time on a famous author. This seems to have been for her the happiest period of her career and the most successful and glamorous time of her life. She led a very active social life and she was photographed by the celebrated surrealist Man Ray and for *Vogue* magazine. In 1928 she wrote a light-hearted and very popular novel, *Orlando*.

In 1931 she published the most unusual and most 'difficult' of her novels, *The Waves,* and after years of hard struggle and great uncertainty she reverted to a much more traditional form for *The*

Years which was published in 1937. Her last novel, *Between the Acts*, was published posthumously in 1941. In that year she killed herself by drowning in a river near her house in Sussex.

Virginia Woolf's output as a writer was very large. Apart from her novels and many short stories she also wrote several books of essays on literature, a biography of her friend Roger Fry, and two books about the position of women in society. The first of these, *A Room of One's Own* (1929), was written soon after *To the Lighthouse* and is very relevant to some of the themes of this novel. In it she argues for women's autonomy and financial independence and she traces the history of some of the obstacles that have stood in the way of women becoming writers – the fact that they have been denied education, the demands made on them by marriage and family life, and the cultural norm of the self-sacrificing woman whose role is always to be attentive to the needs of others (a figure she referred to as 'the angel in the house' and who bears a strong resemblance to Mrs Ramsay).

Virginia Woolf's second book on the subject of women's role in society was *Three Guineas* (1938) and in this she argued that professional women should remain 'outsiders' and should refuse to be drawn into the dominant male culture, a culture which she saw as arrogant, aggressive and militaristic.

Virginia Woolf also wrote a series of autobiographical papers and memoirs and these have since her death been collected together and published as *Moments of Being*. The most important, as background to *To the Lighthouse,* is the essay in this collection called 'A Sketch of the Past'. There is in addition her diary, published in five volumes, and six volumes of letters. As a result of this mass of material we now have an extremely full and intimate record of her life.

The genesis of *To the Lighthouse* is recorded in both her diary and in 'A Sketch of the Past'. She first thought of the book (in 1925) as being about her father and she had a strong image of him sitting in a boat fishing. As she wrote, the book expanded and became a portrait of both her parents who had had a powerful and emotionally puzzling influence on her long after their deaths. She often had a strong sense of the presence of her mother and she wrote in 'A Sketch of the Past', 'Until I was in the forties . . . the presence of my mother obsessed me. I could hear her voice, see her, imagine what she would do or say as I went about my day's doings.' As for her father, she had intense but ambivalent feelings about him. She respected him and identified with him as a writer.

She seems to have decided at an early age to be a writer and she resented the social convention whereby her brothers were provided with an expensive education at private school and university whereas she had to stay at home. However, her father encouraged her and lent her whatever books she wanted from his library. He took her seriously and talked to her about her reading and writing. She greatly admired his courage as an intellectual and the fact that he was unorthodox and unworldly. On the other hand, he acted the part of patriarch and he was an outrageous tyrant, storming around the house and making demands on his wife and daughters. After Julia Stephen's death he became even more impossible, emotionally indulgent and bullying, especially to Vanessa when she took on the management of the household. Virginia came to see him as an unhappy man who had wanted to be perceived as a genius but who was tormented inside with the knowledge that he was a failure. His reaction to his wife's death was self-dramatising and his children became embarrassed by him. In writing *To the Lighthouse* Virginia Woolf attempted to portray this profound ambivalence toward her father. She wanted to create a synthesis of different perspectives on her parents, to combine within one work both the relationship with them that she and her brothers had had when they were children and also the view of them that she arrived at as an adult.

The novel does not so much attempt to tell the story of her parent's lives or their marriage as to give a sense of their presence, to celebrate them or write a tribute to them. In doing this Virginia Woolf found herself departing so far from the normal techniques of fiction that she wondered if what she was writing was really a novel at all or whether it might not be called an elegy, which is a poetic literary form for memorialising the dead. She believed that to capture in writing what was deeply important in someone's life one should not choose to write biography, for biographies tend to be restricted to the external or merely dramatic events in people's lives. Her view was that the really fundamental experiences that we have are those 'moments of being' or 'moments of vision' when we experience an intense sense of a reality that is normally hidden beneath the cotton wool of our ordinary, everyday experience. Her creation of imaginary moments like this for her parents is the basis of *To the Lighthouse*. She believed that her own life was built upon her strongly enduring memories of those childhood holidays in Cornwall, and upon one in particular which she thought was her most important memory:

It is of lying half asleep, half awake, in bed in the nursery at St. Ives. It was of hearing the waves breaking, one, two, one, two, and sending a splash of water over the beach; and then breaking, one, two, one, two, behind a yellow blind. It is of hearing the blind draw its little acorn across the floor as the wind blew the blind out.

It is of lying and hearing this splash and seeing this light, and feeling, it is almost impossible that I should be here; of feeling the purest ecstasy I can conceive. ('A Sketch of the Past')

Intense moments like this, though they survive in us, are very hard to bring clearly to consciousness. It is as though they are, at least sometimes, so fleeting when experienced that we hardly have a chance to explore and appreciate them properly, but are very hard to recapture clearly and fully in memory and are therefore tantalising or haunting. One of Virginia Woolf's aims as a writer was to attempt to bring these moments into focus and then to stabilise them and fill them out in words. This is why often in her novels experience seems to happen in slow motion so that significant moments can be expanded and their full meaning and quality can be appreciated. It is in this sense that *To the Lighthouse* is autobiographical. Virginia Woolf wrote in her diary in March 1925, as she was starting her work on *To the Lighthouse*, 'The past is beautiful because one never realises an emotion at the time. It expands later, and thus we don't have complete emotions about the present, only about the past.

2 SUMMARIES AND
CRITICAL COMMENTARY

2.1 OVERALL SUMMARY

Page references in brackets are to the Panther paperback edition
published by Granada (London, 1977).

Part 1   The Window

The Ramsay family and guests are staying on holiday on the Isle of
Skye in Scotland. It is the middle of September, some time before the
First World War. Mrs Ramsay promises her son James that there will
be a trip to the lighthouse across the bay the next day if the weather is
fine. Mr Ramsay infuriates his son by asserting gruffly that the
weather will not in fact be fine. The narration of this little exchange is
interspersed with the narration of the thoughts and feelings, memories and perceptions of the characters. The reader rapidly gets a sense
of the main characters and their relationships.

   All of Part I takes place on this one day and relates the comings
and goings of the holiday party. Mr Ramsay talks to his young
colleague Charles Tansley and walks up and down the garden
worrying about being a failure. Two guests, Lily Briscoe and William
Bankes, walk and talk and Lily paints a picture. Another guest,
Augustus Carmichael, dozes in a chair on the lawn. A group of
Ramsay children and friends have gone down to the beach where
Paul Rayley and Minta Doyle will become engaged. The main focus
of this Part is on Mrs Ramsay and on her relationship with her
husband and son. In the evening she presides over a large, successful
dinner party. The Part ends with Mr and Mrs Ramsay sitting together
and reading late in the evening.

Part II   Time Passes

Ten years pass by. The family does not visit the house and it becomes
neglected and gradually falls into a state of disrepair. The focus of the
narration in this Part is on the passage of time and on the processes of
nature which continue with their changes and their rhythms, indifferent to the absence or the fate of human beings. There are reported in
parentheses, as if they were facts of little consequence, a series of
deaths in the Ramsay family. Mrs Ramsay dies suddenly one night.
Prue her daughter dies in childbirth. Andrew Ramsay is killed by a
shell, for the First World War is taking place. At last Mrs McNab the
cleaner receives a message that the family is to visit the house again.
She, together with Mrs Bast and her son, set about cleaning and
repairing the house and garden and putting everything in order. The
Part ends as the guests arrive for the visit.

Part III   The Lighthouse

The events narrated in this Part take place on one day ten years later
than Part I. Mr Ramsay has decided that there will be a boat trip to
the lighthouse. His son and daughter, James and Cam, now teen-
agers, are to go with him. Lily Briscoe spends the day painting on the
lawn where another guest, Augustus Carmichael, again dozes in a
chair. During the day various things are accomplished – the trip to
the lighthouse, Lily's painting – and they enable the characters each
to come to terms with Mrs Ramsay's death and with each other.

2.2   SECTION SUMMARIES AND CRITICAL COMMENTARY

Part 1   section 1 (9–19)

Mrs Ramsay and her six-year-old son James are sitting at the window
of the family holiday house. James is cutting illustrations from a
catalogue while his mother knits stockings for the lighthouse keeper's
son in case the trip to the lighthouse should take place the next day.
Mr Ramsay, who does not believe in tailoring the facts to anybody's
wishes, announces that the trip will not be possible. A young disciple,
Charles Tansley, agrees with him. Mrs Ramsay finds young Tansley
odious but she keeps this to herself and tries to make things easy for
him. She thinks that it is a woman's duty to protect and look after
men. She approves of their power in the world and likes to be trusted
and worshipped by them.

She and Tansley set off to walk to the nearby town. She is to visit a family where there is illness. As they walk they view some of the aspects of the scene that will gradually take on varying degrees of symbolic significance as the novel progresses, the bay, the sea, the lighthouse and the sand dunes. Tansley comes to feel a strong attraction to Mrs Ramsay. He finds her very beautiful and is proud to be with her.

Some of the narration relates conversation among the characters in direct quotation, but far more of it relates their thoughts, perceptions, memories, feelings, and so on, i.e. their inner, subjective lives. The point of view of the narration shifts from one character to another and the reader needs to keep in mind which character's inner, subjective experiences are being reported at each point. Moreover, the narration also shifts about in time. There is a main time framework to which the narration always returns, but interspersed along it there are flashbacks which keep the reader informed of past episodes which have a bearing on the significance of present events. Furthermore, some of the narration does not relate particular past events but rather events which have been repeated in the past and which are typical of characters' ways of behaving or thinking. For example, we are told not that Mrs Ramsay did once ask her children to imagine what it must be like to be a lighthouse keeper but that she *would* do this, which is to say that she was in the habit of doing it.

By these means the reader gradually builds up a dense and complex sense of the characters and of what is at stake when they talk to one another. The narration moves very smoothly and subtly from one character to another, from their external actions and conversations to their inner experiences, and from one time to another. The reader has to learn how to follow these movements.

Part 1   section 2 (19)

Tansley's loyalties are now divided between Mr and Mrs Ramsay. Imitating Mr Ramsay, he again warns James that there will be no trip to the lighthouse tomorrow, but he attempts to soften his tone so that he will not earn Mrs Ramsay's displeasure. His effort to please both Ramsay parents is clumsy and Mrs Ramsay strongly dislikes him.

Part 1   section 3 (19–21)

This section is narrated throughout from Mrs Ramsay's point of view. It is a little later in the day. Mrs Ramsay is again sitting with James. She tries to cheer him up by telling him that the weather may after all turn out to be fine next day. At one moment the background sounds of domestic life happen to cease and she becomes aware of the sound of the waves. Her mood changes and her thoughts turn towards the passage of time. She experiences a moment of terror before becoming reimmersed in the flow of the day's ordinary activities. Suddenly Mr Ramsay, who has been marching up and down the terrace, shouts out 'Stormed at with shot and shell'. He has been reciting Tennyson's poem 'The Charge of the Light Brigade' to himself and has become carried away in his excitement.

Part I   section 4 (21–8)

At the end of the previous section Mrs Ramsay looked up and saw Lily Briscoe, who is doing a painting of her. Mr Ramsay, absorbed in his poem, almost walks into her easel. In a typical move the narration comes back to the same scene but now relates it from a new angle. It shifts to Lily's point of view.

William Bankes joins Lily and they swap views about Mr Ramsay. The narration shifts from one point of view to the other during their conversation. In her own mind Lily is worrying about her painting. She lacks confidence and would like to confide in Mrs Ramsay. They stroll off and are exhilarated by the sea and the waves. The sand dunes remind William Bankes of walks that he took with Mr Ramsay when they were young and he frets about their friendship. As they return they encounter a Ramsay daughter, Cam, who is seven, who rebuffs Bankes's attempt to befriend her. We encounter in these passages a theme which is pondered by several of the characters, the relative merits and attractions of marriage and family life as against solitude and privacy. Bankes is a widower and is childless but would like to have had a daughter, but he wonders whether Mr Ramsay was not more impressive when he was a young man before he took on all the burdens of family life and the pleasures of domesticity.

As they talk they try to arrive at an assessment of Mr Ramsay but Lily is aware of how complex and contradictory he is. What it is to know somebody is a problem with which Lily is much preoccupied. To know a person one has to hold together in one's mind very many factors. In Lily's mind they are as numerous as a swarm of gnats, and are held together in a precarious pattern until they are disturbed by Jasper shooting birds and by Mr Ramsay who comes charging through a gap in the hedge declaiming his poem, booming out, 'Someone has blundered!'. He is embarrassed by his blunder, but also defiant. He turns away pretending that he has not seen them, determined not to have his indulgence in the poem's emotions spoiled.

Part I   section 5 (29–32)

We return to Mrs Ramsay. She thinks that Lily Briscoe and William
Bankes should marry for she does not suffer any doubts about the
importance of marriage for a woman. She thinks about her own
domestic scene and becomes irritated with thoughts about the
shabbiness of the house. She remembers that the maid's father is
dying. Mrs Ramsay's thoughts regularly gravitate towards death, so
that when she says, 'It's too short', we are not sure whether she is not
thinking about life as well as about her knitting. Sadness descends
upon her. The point of view of the narrative changes. Mrs Ramsay's
sad looks are described. Gossip and speculation about what it is in her
past that causes her to be so sad are reported. But Mrs Ramsay is
so silent, so uncommunicative about her past, that no-one, not even
the narrator, knows her secrets. She is silent and sad and very beautiful
and to illustrate for us the impression she makes upon men we are
given in parentheses an account of William Bankes's extravagant
feelings for her. Bankes thinks that it is incongruous that a woman of
such regal beauty should do anything so banal as to talk on the
telephone about trains. The tone is ironic, mocking Bankes's stereotyped thoughts about Mrs Ramsay.

Part I   section 6 (32–8)

Mrs Ramsay remembers that she had heard her husband blurting out
'Someone had blundered' and turns to see that he is still suffering
embarrassment and distress. She transfers the feeling of tenderness
that this elicits in her onto James. The competition between James
and his father, who both want to receive Mrs Ramsay's attentions, is
a key feature of the afternoon's emotional dramas. Mr Ramsay stops
for a word with his wife only to reactivate James's hatred. The trip to
the lighthouse is mentioned again and now Mr Ramsay is so outraged
by what he perceives as his wife's irrationality that he angrily curses
her. Mrs Ramsay seems to be a willing victim of this verbal violence.
She respects her husband's uncompromising assertiveness and submits
uncomplainingly to his abuse.

   Mr Ramsay walks away and resumes his meditations about his
career as a philosopher which he thinks of as a journey through the
alphabet. He has made his way to Q and now must press on to R. His
habit of self-dramatisation is comically demonstrated as he imagines
himself to be a hero, the leader of a dangerous expedition. In spite of
these inflated self-images, Mr Ramsay feels himself threatened by a
sense of failure. He worries that his fame will not long outlive him.
He longs to go to his wife for comfort.

Part I   section 7 (38–41)

James sees his father approaching and hates his emotionality. He knows that he will take his mother's attentions away from him (she is reading to him a fairy story, 'The Fisherman's Wife'). In one of the most sustained passages of intense, poetic writing in the novel, Mrs Ramsay becomes a fountain of energy which washes warmly over her husband. She sympathises, she reassures, she soothes. James is left neglected and feeling impotent and angry. Mrs Ramsay is left exhausted, emptied, and ill at ease with a feeling of being superior to her husband. Mr Ramsay is in general scornful of her exaggerations and thinks of them as typical of women's incapacity to deal with things truthfully. But his wife knows that her reassurance of him is built upon exaggeration and upon lies.

Part I   section 8 (41–6)

Mrs Ramsay thinks about Augustus Carmichael and his life. He is one of the few people who can resist liking Mrs Ramsay in spite of her efforts to win him over and he discomforts her. He undermines the sense that she has of her own worth. It is as if he can see through all her self-sacrificing attentions to other people and can see her real self-serving motives underneath. Mrs Ramsay carries on reading the story to James and her mind is able simultaneously to pursue various trains of thought.

Mr Ramsay passes by. He is still thinking about fame. He is now thinking less selfishly, trying to put together some thoughts for a lecture. It is when he is like this, absorbed in his thinking and undistracted by trivialities, like a sentinel guarding against the approach of falsehood, that he inspires in those who see him feelings of reverence. But in fact his mind returns to his obsession with his own failure and to the continual need that he has to disguise his real feelings. In public he has to pretend to be indifferent to praise and fame. He is (in a strikingly modern phrase) 'afraid to own his own feelings'.

The section ends with Lily Briscoe who is packing up her paints and thinking about Mr Ramsay.

Part I   section 9 (46–53)

Lily Briscoe and William Bankes discuss Mr and Mrs Ramsay. Each of them loves Mrs Ramsay, though in different ways. They look at her sitting in the window with James, posing for Lily's painting.

Bankes is enraptured. Lily tries to resist being carried away with her feelings for the Ramsays. She is very excited by Bankes's intoxication with Mrs Ramsay. When she looks at her painting which was meant to capture some of this intensity she finds that it is a complete failure. Her exalted mood destroyed, Lily thinks more about Mrs Ramsay and begins to build a more complicated and shadowed picture of her in her mind. She is not perfect. She can be domineering and rather narrow. Lily remembers how Mrs Ramsay had come to her room late one night and had a long talk with her about marriage. Lily had found Mrs Ramsay's certainty, her complete unwillingness to allow any doubt about marriage being the central meaning of a woman's life, inflexible and oppressive. Lily had longed for intimacy with Mrs Ramsay, with that closeness with another person which is like a merging with them. Intimacy is a repeated theme in the novel. Lily in particular longs for it but finds it puzzling and sometimes frightening because she also has a strong need for solitude and privacy. People attempt to achieve it in different ways, they have illusions about love and about each other. Part I will end with Mr and Mrs Ramsay sharing a moment of intimacy together, almost as if this were the end towards which the whole day, with its dramas of aggression and reconciliation, sharing and solitude, was striving.

The narration returns to the main time-line as Bankes initiates a conversation about Lily's painting. He is respectful and willing to listen to her explanations. Her painting is both a tribute to Mrs Ramsay and yet organised by abstract aesthetic principles (mass, colour, line, and so on). It is contrasted with the prevailing sentimentalist aesthetic norms of the fictional Mr Paunceforte. The principles and problems of Lily's painting which is a tribute to Mrs Ramsay are not far removed from those of Virginia Woolf's novel which is a tribute to her parents. In Part II and its climax we will gain an even stronger sense of this parallel.

Part I   section 10 (53–60)

Cam, who is dashing wildly around the garden, goes past Lily Briscoe and Willian Bankes and on to her mother. She forms a bridge between sections 9 and 10, as if she were picking up the narration from the couple on the lawn and carrying it over to the window for her mother to take it up. Mrs Ramsay also picks up Lily's topic, marriage; she is reading to James about the fairy tale fisherman and his wife and at the same time she thinks about the young couple Paul Rayley and Minta Doyle whom she wants to see engaged.

Mrs Ramsay also finds her thoughts turning, as so often, to time and its passing, her children growing up, suffering and death. There is some connection between her own tragic experiences and her commitment to working for the poor and the sick. Her desire that people should marry and have children is also connected to her pessimism about life but she is aware that she could be accused of being too forceful. The things about Mrs Ramsay which section 9 related from Lily's point of view are now in section 10 told again, this time from Mrs Ramsay's own point of view. Even so we still come up against that barrier of silence and sadness at the heart of her, for when her thoughts turn towards her own past tragedy she carefully does not name it, not even to herself. Her silence is self-protective; she cannot bear to remember.

She finishes reading the story to James and looks up and sees that the lighthouse beam is shining. As so often, this final paragraph of the section both rounds off the section smoothly and provides a bridge to the following section. The lighthouse is to be a central character in section 11.

Part 1   section 11 (60–3)

It is early evening. The bustle and business of the day have faded away and Mrs Ramsay is by herself for the first time. As all the attachments to people and activities fall away she sinks back to a peaceful dark core of herself, swayed by the rhythm of the lighthouse beam, until she finds herself hypnotised into a ritual incantation, 'We are in the hands of the Lord', a phrase which is false to her sense of pessimism. She relaxes into a semi-dreamlike state. Images float into her mind. The lighthouse beam becomes like a ghostly presence that hypnotises her and caresses her, climaxing in ecstasy and delight. She has moved from the gloom of 'It will end' to the satisfaction of 'It is enough'.

This section gives a striking picture of the way in which Mrs Ramsay's mind not only moves from one object of attention to another but actually takes on quite different states. It is as if different selves live together in her and take over from one another in different circumstances. When she asks who had said 'We are in the hands of the Lord', it is because some other self had surfaced in her. Her mind is no longer under the control of the active, practical intelligence which is operating when she is busy nor the intuitive emotional empathy which is engaged when she is responding to her husband's demands. She exists more through her body and its semi-conscious responsiveness to the rhythms of the lighthouse and the power of those rhythms to conjure up images, phrases and feelings. In attempting to depict this state of mind the prose becomes lyrical, song-like and dense with metaphor. Like dream images, the images which rise up off the floor of Mrs Ramsay's mind are very suggestive of powerful latent meanings, and have strong feeling attached to them. They are erotic, even orgasmic.

Mr Ramsay sees his wife sitting silently by herself and finds her lovely. He decides not to interrupt her privacy, but she goes to him without being asked, aware of his desire.

Part I   section 12 (63–8)

Mr and Mrs Ramsay stroll together in the garden. In earlier sections conversations between them have been related in a kind of slow motion, with a great deal of reporting on the inner mental activity interspersed between the actual spoken words. In the previous section there was almost no speech or activity at all and the narration was almost entirely taken up with Mrs Ramsay's solitary, disengaged inner life. By contrast, in section 12 she has come right back to the surface and as she chats with Mr Ramsay there is very little simulta-neous inner thinking and debating going on. This relaxed, easy chatter between husband and wife does not seem to have a great weight of meaning behind it. Therefore, the narration of their conversation accelerates. Far more often than before the narration employs the traditional novelistic dialogue conventions of direct and indirect quotation.

At a certain point in their conversation, however, when Mr Ramsay tells her that he does not like to see her look sad, there is the possibility of it going deeper, of Mrs Ramsay sharing some of her more intimate thoughts with her husband. But this she refuses to do. She cannot share with him the ecstasy she had felt while watching the lighthouse beam. Her reticence sets limits to their intimacy and this causes them to move apart again into their own trains of thought.

Part I   section 13 (68–70)

Lily Briscoe and William Bankes are also strolling in the garden and chatting easily together. Lily sees the Ramsays together and finds that at that moment they seem not so much like a couple of complex people but have become abstract and symbolical, signifying marriage.

They all watch Prue and Jasper play ball and Mrs Ramsay asks Prue whether those who went to the beach have returned yet and whether Nancy had gone with them. This question will be left hanging in the air like the ball that the children are throwing up until it is caught by Prue in section 15, which is a typical example of Virginia Woolf's witty play with the conventions of the novel.

Part I section 14 (70–4)

The whole of this section is within parentheses. The narrative moves away in both time and space from the main narrative line, for it is a flashback, which tells the story of Nancy's and Andrew's trip to the beach with Paul Rayley and Minta Doyle. This pair do become engaged as Mrs Ramsay had hoped. As they return Minta loses her brooch.

Part I section 15 (75)

Prue Ramsay answers her mother's question and the main narrative time-line is thereby re-established.

Part I section 16 (75–8)

We rejoin Mrs Ramsay who has gone to her room to dress for dinner. It is to be a special dinner tonight because William Bankes has agreed to eat with them and the cook has spent three days preparing a special dish. Mrs Ramsay and her children watch the rooks outside in the trees, which gives Mrs Ramsay an opportunity to indulge her liking for fantasy and story telling (which Jasper, being male, scornfully rejects). As the late-comers arrive back from the beach downstairs Mrs Ramsay regally, ceremonially descends the stairs as if this were all preparation for some special performance, which indeed it is. The author adopts here a tone of affectionate mockery at Mrs Ramsay's self-consciously courtly performance, a tone which is common throughout the book.

Part I section 17 (78–103)

This is the longest section in the novel and it is a great set piece, the dinner party, the scene of Mrs Ramsay's creative triumph. By her efforts and skill the fragmented and jaded collection of people will be brought together into a temporary state of harmony, well-being and togetherness. At the beginning each of the company is weary, frustrated or dissatisfied. They are indifferent or aggressive to each other. Even William Bankes finds his rapture for Mrs Ramsay has vanished. Lily Briscoe and Charles Tansley irritate each other. Mrs

Ramsay thinks of the party as like a ship setting out on a sea voyage possibly heading for disaster. The narration moves from one character to another. They are each preoccupied with some private train of thought. At a certain point so strong is Mrs Ramsay's sense that everything is wrong and that the ship is heading for disaster that she, without speaking, appeals to Lily to help her out. For it is the social convention that it is the woman's role to navigate on these occasions, by paying attention to the needs of men and giving them plenty of opportunity to exercise their vanity. At this point, life and warmth begin to flow into the party.

The meal is all about female creativity. Mrs Ramsay with Lily's help creates warmth and conviviality. Mildred, the cook has created the special main dish, *boeuf en daube*, and Rose has created a beautiful arrangement with the fruit bowl. In each case the achievement is a matter of careful and sensitive arrangements and combinations of separate components into a blended whole. In each case the resulting beauty is temporary; the arrangements do not last. However, this does not negate their value. They are enjoyed and moreover they will survive in people's memory. People, lives, marriages, meals, childhood – these are all achievements, patterns or arrangements which last for some time and then pass away. The marriage of Paul Rayley and Minta Doyle, which is another of Mrs Ramsay's creations, will, as we shall see in Part III, not turn out to be a success. As for Paul's love for Minta, this sparks off in Lily a typical ambivalence, for she both intensely desires to have a share in this experience but also finds it frightening and destructive.

The dinner party is like a container which can hold peacefully together many different things. It brings together different people. It can also contain and hold in a harmonious pattern different layers of consciousness, different selves. Some exhanges are at a level of apparently purely superficial courtesy, while others are serious and substantial conversations. There is a place for both chat about the food and for agonising about the nature of love, for a discussion of fishermen's wages and a recital of verse. The narration of the dinner party, in which all these things are eventually smoothly contained in one seamless fabric of prose, is just as much a creative triumph as the dinner party itself. There is a peaceful coexistence of the superficial and the profound, as for example: 'It partook, she felt, carefully helping Mr Bankes to a specially tender piece, or eternity.'

'But how long do you think it will last?', somebody asks, and this discordant note (which will destroy the relaxed atmosphere by reminding Mr Ramsay of the anxiety-ridden subject of his fame) also signals the beginning of the end for the dinner party. It is a reminder that it too is doomed to last but a little while. Somebody takes some fruit and destroys the beauty of Rose's arrangement of the fruit bowl, and Mrs Ramsay now feels anxious, for this has made her think of her children, especially of Prue, and of their uncertain future. In a last burst of warmth before the party ends, Mr Ramsay and Mr Carmichael recite a poem ('Come out and climb the garden path' by Charles Elton). The poem seems to speak for Mrs Ramsay, to be articulating her pleasure and relief. They rise to go their separate ways. As she leaves the room Mrs Ramsay pauses for a moment on the threshold and looks back as if to preserve for just one moment this vanishing scene as it fades away into the past.

Part I   section 18 (103–8)

Mrs Ramsay leaves and the party breaks up. As she goes up the stairs she assesses her achievement. She has created something that will survive in memory, that people will not forget as she has not forgotten her own parents. She has created a community of feeling. This form of togetherness which gives her such satisfaction is in strong contrast to other forms of intimacy that have been debated in the course of the day – the merging that Lily desired, the consuming heat of sexual passion that is foretold in the engagement, the violation of barriers in the sharing of secrets that Mrs Ramsay had rejected with her husband. Mrs Ramsay's image is a very striking one: she thinks of the walls of partition that divide people having become so thin that their experience had become all one stream, a stream that would continue after her death. This is also a good metaphor for this novel itself – a collective stream of consciousness.

Mrs Ramsay goes to see her youngest children. Cam is afraid of a boar's skull that is nailed to the wall and needs to be comforted with fairy stories. James wants the skull left where it is, so his mother covers it with her shawl to hide it from Cam. These moments will also survive in memory long after her death, as we shall see in Part III.

Part I   section 19 (108–14)

Mr and Mrs Ramsay sit quietly together reading. Mr Ramsay loses his anxieties as he reads a novel by Sir Walter Scott. Mrs Ramsay reads a Shakespeare sonnet and finds that it collects together and articulates the separate parts of her experience. As they chat together they achieve a kind of easy intimacy. Mr Ramsay wants his wife to tell him that she loves him but her deep reticence will not permit her to do this. Nevertheless, she wordlessly conveys her love by looking at him and smiling. The Part ends on a note of a reconciliation and happiness.

Part II   sections 1 and 2 (117–18)

The time-line of Part I gradually runs down as the various characters go to bed. When they are all asleep and it is dark and silent, a different time framework takes over, the time of natural processes. Winds and draughts blow around the house. There are slight movements among the flowers, a door slams. By the end of section 2 it is clear that in this time framework human beings and their activities are only of marginal significance. This is registered by the fact that they are narrated within brackets, as when at the end of section 2, in the last little flurry of activity left over from Part I, Mr Carmichael puts out his light.

Part II   section 3 (119–20)

The narration is now firmly established in a non-human perspective. The tense is continuous present. The word 'now' does not refer to some one moment but to the whole season, ('The nights now are full of wind'). The marginal story of human lives again appears fleetingly within brackets: we learn that Mrs Ramsay has died.

Part II   section 4 (120–1)

The house is empty and what used to be the scene of human life is now entirely given over to natural processes. The movements of air and light are now so slight as to be almost eventless, except that very, very slowly things are changing, a board springs up, Mrs Ramsay's shawl falls loose. Mrs McNab arrives to clean and air the house.

Part II   section 5 (121–2)

We are given a portrait of the witless and toothless Mrs McNab as she cleans the house. Though she is presented as scarcely human (and the portrait might well be found offensive) she has also, it seems, experienced the joys and sadnesses of a human life and feels some mixture of lamentation and hope.

A strange and unexplained mystic and visionary presence appears on the beach asking for explanations.

Part II   section 6 (122–5)

Spring and summer. Prue Ramsay marries but then dies in childbirth. There is a season of mysterious distant explosions, for the Great War has broken out. The processes of nature continue, silent, indifferent. Andrew Ramsay is killed. The visionaries walking on the beach are disturbed by signs that some awful catastrophe has occured, that make it impossible for them to continue peacefully with their lyric visions. Nature is disfigured by the distant violence: 'there was a purplish stain upon the bland surface of the sea as if something had boiled and bled invisibly beneath.' Mr Carmichael publishes a book of poems.

Part II   section 7 (125–6)

Nature is blind and indifferent. It is shapeless, for there is nothing to provide order whether in the tumult of winter or the stillness of spring. These idiot games, that produce nothing but brute confusion, may also be the continuing war which destroys all possibility of civilisation and human meaning.

Part II   section 8 (126–7)

There is a turning point, and the beginning of a return to a human time framework and human perspectives. The narration is from Mrs McNab's point of view. She cleans the house. Some events reappear not now marginalised within brackets but within Mrs McNab's consciousness. She thinks about the deaths in the Ramsay family and comes across the death's emblem of the boar's skull in the children's bedroom.

Part II   section 9 (128–31)

The destruction and the fertility of nature continue. The abandoned house is on the very point of complete destruction. Mrs McNab is defeated. A message arrives announcing that the Ramsays are to visit and the house is saved. Mrs McNab, Mrs Bast and her son painfully reestablish human order. After huge effort their creativity triumphs. The house is restored to order. 'It was finished'. (These are the very same words that will announce the completion of Lily's painting at the end of the novel.) For the last time the insensibility of nature is interruped by brackets; Lily Briscoe and Mr Carmichael arrive.

Part II   section 10 (132–3)

This section reestablishes the points of view of the characters. Lily hears waves; Mr Carmichael reads. As the night passes we know that it is in preparation for the reappearance of human consciousness. The section and Part II ends as Lily wakes in the morning.

Part III   section 1 (137–41)

Ten years have passed. Lily Briscoe is forty years old. She has not married. Her emotions at being back among the Ramsays are confused. Mr Ramsay is angry waiting for his recalcitrant children to get ready for a trip to the lighthouse. Lily decides to spend the day painting. She had never solved the problems of composition that her painting of Mrs Ramsay had set all those years ago. She finds it is impossible to work with Mr Ramsay pacing around demanding sympathy, just as he used to do when his wife was alive.

This first section introduces us to the events that are to play the major role in this Part, the long-awaited trip to the lighthouse and Lily's painting. As they progress each of the characters will be coming to terms with the death of Mrs Ramsay and with their relationships with Mr Ramsey.

Part III   section 2 (141–6)

Mr Ramsay and Lily Briscoe confront one another on the lawn. His demands are a challenge to Lily's femininity and she feels inadequate because she cannot respond as convention says that a woman should. Mr Ramsay is at his most posturing and self-dramatising. They are rescued from their situation of mutual dissatisfaction by discovering in Mr Ramsay's boots some emotionally safe common ground of interest on which to make sympathetic contact. Lily can allow herself to feel some affection for him without being submerged. The children arrive and they set off on their trip.

Part III   section 3 (146–51)

As Lily begins to paint her mind relaxes into a detached, submerged state that allows her thoughts to roam freely, out of her control. Thoughts appear in her mind rising up from the depths. Her painting is performed almost as if her body were obeying its own rhythms, like dancing. She remembers a scene on the beach (which is new to the reader). Mrs Ramsay is writing letters and talking with Tansley. It must have been one of those special 'moments of being' that, because they somehow make concrete an emotion and hold together with particular clarity and power our sense of a person for whom we care, stay in the mind, a satisfying vision like a work of art. There is, Lily believes, no great revelation which encompasses everything and reveals the meaning of life. There are only these moments of illumination which survive in the mind.

Lily walks to the edge of the lawn and watches the boat set out on its journey, shrouded in profound silence, like a funeral ceremony.

Part III   section 4 (151–8)

The focus in this section is the thoughts and feelings of the two children who share an angry resentment at their father's tyrannical ways. Mr Ramsay and Macalister the boatman talk about the great storm which had wrecked ships here in the bay the previous year. Macalister's son fishes for mackerel. As the journey gets under way, Cam and James begin to separate, to each have their different reactions to their father. Cam finds that she is proud of her father and the tie between brother and sister slackens.

Mr Ramsay has sunk into a day dream and with his usual embarrassing emotional intensity he blurts out mournful lines of poetry (from William Cowper's 'The Castaway'). He attempts to charm Cam, to win her over, and James can see that she is torn between her loyalty to him and her love for her father. Watching Cam's face sparks off in James's mind some memory of his mother. He begins to explore his memories of his parents and this fuels his rage at his father. Some very important process of clarification, of forming a layer of identity, is under way in James. His relationship with his father is blocked by this great anger which must be resolved.

Part III   section 5 (158–67)

Lily works away on her painting and simultaneously on her memories of Mrs Ramsay. So many of Mrs Ramsay's projects have come to nothing. Lily has not married William Bankes though they have remained friends. The Rayleys' marriage has not been a success. But she thinks of Mrs Ramsay silent on the beach, uncommunicative, and wonders what it is to know another person. People change, time passes, so the perspective that people who are now dead had on things necessarily becomes more and more dated and distant. The dead fade away from us. As she thinks these things Lily finds that her mind has risen to the surface so that she has lost that state of unconsciousness of her surroundings, that state of absorption, that is necessary when painting. She is back on the lawn and feeling misery. Words fail her and she is threatened by overwhelming emotion. Her anguish at the loss of Mrs Ramsay breaks through. She turns to Carmichael but he is dozing in his chair. Lily's grief is caught in a wonderful series of images – a hand with a knife seems to express her sense of being wounded bodily. She is surprised by the strength of her emotion and feels that life is not safe if one can be suddenly overtaken by something with such force. She feels out of control, as if she had jumped from the top of a tower.

Part III   section 6 (167)

In a startling move, the narrative here suddenly turns again to the boat, where Macalister's boy cuts a square out of the side of a fish with his knife and throws it, mutilated but still alive, back into the sea. The brief section is in square brackets and is itself like a hole which has been cut into the text. Its purpose is not to advance the story of what is happening in the boat but to provide a metaphor and a strong visual image that depicts what Lily feels but cannot herself express in words – that she is at a loss, pained and disoriented by grief.

Part III   section 7 (167–9)

Lily, surprised by the violence of her grief, cries out, but immediately feels embarrassed and humiliated. Gradually the pain subsides. Carmichael did not notice that she had cried out, that she had metaphorically stepped off a plank and fallen into the sea. She has a sense of Mrs Ramsay's presence there in the garden. She returns to her painting. She has a comforting vision, that she has often experienced before, of Mrs Ramsay with a wreath of white flowers walking across the fields. She notices the Ramsay's boat now halfway across the bay.

Part III   section 8 (169–73)

In the boat the children are immersed in their memories. Cam's mind wanders in an underwater world where it encounters a ghostly presence shrouded in a green cloak (recalling Mrs Ramsay's green shawl draped over the boar's skull). James concentrates on his father's gestures which he associates with a memory of the stabbing and jabbing movements with which his father had prodded his leg when he was a little boy. Sitting now, as he had when he sat with his mother all those years ago, in a posture of impotent rage, James's desire to strike his father with a knife is revived. But now he begins to resolve his angry vision, to see that he can distinguish between the figure of tyranny which he hates so fiercely and his father, who is also a sad old man who can be quite kindly and who can become so excited about the fisherman and their sports. He has begun to understand and respect his father's austerity and to identify with him, to share his values. These two feelings, the fierce hatred and the companionable admiration, are both alive in him. He tries to trace the hatred to its source, to discover the original scene of his father's insensitivity, and as he sinks down into his memories he comes upon a rustling dress and women's voices and the yellow eye of the lighthouse. He remembers his father's aggression as having been like a wheel which crushed his mother's foot. The lighthouse he can see now is a stark black and white tower. We arrive at a point of extreme tension in which it seems something must break. The boat is motionless, becalmed, and James is trapped in his web of contradictory emotions and feels that he cannot move unless he takes a knife and relieves his feelings. At this moment the wind returns, the boat moves and James is released.

Part III   section 9 (174)

The section is a parallel to the short section 6. Again it is in square brackets and interrupts the narrative to provide an image. In section 6 an image derived from the boat was used to express Lily's grief. Here, an image derived from the island, where Lily stands looking out to sea, expresses James's misery. It is an image of separation. He had felt abandoned by his mother when she had turned away from him to attend to his father when he was a little boy. No doubt he had felt abandoned by her again when she died. He can now defuse his rage at those abandonments and watch his mother fade away into the distance. A sad ceremony of farewell is in progress; the vanished steamer's smoke 'drooped like a flag mournfully in valediction'.

Part III   section 10 (174–6)

Cam looks back at the island. For her also the anger and the anguish have faded away. She can feel the adventure of life and a great affection for her father. He can be gentle and kind and interested in her. She has a little imaginary dialogue with James in which their conflicting feelings are expressed. Now it is the positive feelings for their father which dominate in her mind and she is happy and relaxed.

Part III   section 11 (176–86)

Lily is also feeling satisfaction and contentment. However, she discovers that there is still something wrong with her picture, that there is some problem with the design which she has not solved. She sits down and thinks about old Carmichael and his strained relationship with Mrs Ramsay. Her mind drifts among her memories and she returns to a favourite preoccupation, how one can never know anybody else, that one would need fifty pairs of eyes to gain different points of view in order to do justice to Mrs Ramsay (and this, of course, is exactly what the novel has itself been attempting, to contain a portrait of Mr and Mrs Ramsay as they are seen from many different points of view).

Lily's mind runs over image after image, scene after scene, trying to contain all her impressions and feelings for Mrs Ramsay, to avoid oversimplified or sentimentalised summaries of her. So she remembers the angers and resentments, the exhaustion and the reconciliations. She returns to her painting with a sense that now she can solve her problem, but she is stabbed again by grief. She has a very clear vision of Mrs Ramsay sitting in the window knitting.

Part III   section 12 (186–91)

The boat nears the lighthouse. James finds that it expresses for him something about his character, a manliness that he shares with his father with whom he now feels at ease. Cam feels safe with her father and able to allow her mind to wander, to enjoy herself inventing stories (as her mother used to do). Mr Ramsay chats with the boatman and dispenses sandwiches. Suddenly he praises James for his handling of the boat. James has at last obtained his father's approval. He has been waiting for this a very long time.

There is a sense of accomplishment as the boat at last arrives at the lighthouse. Mr Ramsay looks back at the blue shape of the island in some private ceremony of farewell to his wife and then leaps like a young man onto the rock.

Part III   section 13 (191–2)

As the boat party reaches its destination, Lily also stares into the distance where the lighthouse melts away into a blue haze. She returns to her picture and as if suddenly clear about the solution that she has been seeking she decisively draws a line in the centre. The painting is also finished.

3 THEMES AND ISSUES

Virginia Woolf herself remarked that very little happens in *To the Lighthouse*. It is not a dramatic novel. Moreover, it does not tell the story of the gradual development of the characters and their lives, culminating in decisive events, like marriage, inheritance or death, which are the events which many traditional novels lead up to. Mrs Ramsay shares with the Victorian novel a belief in marriage, seeing it as the crucial event on which a woman's life is built. In *To the Lighthouse* two marriages do take place but neither of them is of central importance in the novel. Prue Ramsay marries, but she dies soon afterwards in childbirth. Paul Rayley marries Minta Doyle. Their marriage turns out badly and this is an ironic comment on the dated literary convention that all a heroine's problems are over once she is safely wed. Similarly, although there are deaths in the novel, they are not the culminating point of the story; indeed, they are announced within brackets in Part II as a deliberate signal that this is not where the main interest lies. Identity is, as we shall see, one of the novel's themes, but it does not take the form of a story about the achievement of a settled identity by means of financial success or inheritance, as was the case in so many nineteenth-century plots.

To the Lighthouse is also very limited in range. If we compare it with great Victorian novels, for example, we see immediately that many things which are traditionally included within the scope of the novel are missing from *To the Lighthouse*. For example, political, social and historical events and processes are neither represented directly nor taken as central issues for debate. The focus is very narrowly on the family life of the Ramsays, and anything which happens away from their domestic scene is ignored. The most striking example of this is the First World War which occurs in the span of time covered by Part II of the novel. Even though it has dreadful consequences for the Ramsay family (their son Andrew is killed in the trenches) it is not explicitly narrated or discussed. The men at the dinner party in Part I do discuss political and social issues (such as the level of fishermen's wages) but their discussion is not narrated for us. As with all the other possible topics of inquiry (political change, class, modernisation, and so on) the novel very strictly refuses to take an interest.

If we think of how important the theme of social administration is in Dickens's novels or that of politics and class in the novels of George Eliot, we realise just how narrow *To the Lighthouse* is. Similarly if we think of some of Virginia Woolf's contemporaries, such as D.H. Lawrence or Thomas Mann, we are equally struck by the contrast between their novels and *To the Lighthouse*. For example, had Mr Ramsay been a character in a novel by Thomas Mann, then we would probably have been given an account of his philosophical positions and their importance in the development of European culture. As it is, we have only a comic version of them as they are perceived by Lily Briscoe, a scrubbed kitchen table hanging in a pear tree.

This narrowness is a result of a deliberate choice by the author and is not a reflection of her own range of interests. Virginia Woolf was herself fascinated by at least some aspects of politics and history as some of her books, notably *A Room of One's Own* and *Three Guineas*, clearly show. She chose to limit the scope of *To the Lighthouse* because she did not want to be distracted from the main strategy which was to concentrate on some things which have tended to be missing from men's novels. She wanted the focus to be on some areas of life which have been regarded as too boring or too trivial or too simple to be the main subject-matter of fiction. These areas are the subtleties of subjective experience and of family life. The novel deals with the hidden and minute movements of the mind which occur in the course of ordinary, everyday experience. It focuses on the characters in the context of their relationships within the family, between husband and wife, parents and children or within the family circle of friends while at dinner. Although the psychological processes at work within these contexts are not always dramatic they are fundamental to all human personality. They are what allows us to achieve some of the most difficult tasks we face in life; the development of personal identity; the resolution of emotional conflicts within the family; coping with the loss of those we love. These achievements involve the most subtle processes of thought and feeling, and these are often too rapid and too far below the threshold of consciousness for us to be clearly aware of them or for us to be able to put them into words. Virginia Woolf wanted to find ways of representing these kinds of processes, of raising them to the level of verbal expression.

The characters are at the mercy of forces which intrude from outside the domestic circle, notably the forces of nature which kill them (and the war is seen as if it were just another of these indifferent natural forces). The novel's concern is with these two zones and their interaction – the subjective experience of the characters (in Parts I and III) and the forces of nature (in Part II). *To the Lighthouse* confirms Virginia Woolf's belief that the constantly shifting and multilayered subjective experience of people in these contexts is a rich and rewarding field for investigation in a novel.

3.1 PSYCHOLOGICAL THEMES

Identity

One of the most important psychological processes represented in *To the Lighthouse* is the development of identity or a sense of self. We have a strong sense of self if we are clear and confident as to who we are and not plagued by drastic instability or indecision or by fundamental doubts about our worth. In the novel both James Ramsay and Lily Briscoe develop to some degree in this direction.

James, as a six-year-old boy in Part I, is very much attached to his mother, loving her protection and attention and enjoying the fairy stories she reads him. However, he is already different from his sister Cam and more like his father in that he likes to contemplate the undecorated or uncovered truth of the boar's skull which Cam prefers to be hidden by her mother's shawl. In Part III of the novel James has reached a crucial stage in his development. He is old enough to take on more of the identity of an adult man but his progress towards this is blocked by the fierce hatred of his father. He feels wretched because he is trapped or immobilised. It is as if his father held him in a web, and as if the only possibility of progress was in metaphorically killing him, in rejecting him totally. He wants to be able to become more of a man but without becoming utterly hateful as he believes his father to be. He wants none of his father's violent, destructive rages, his self-indulgent emotionality or his insensitivity. His hatred is so powerful that he is prevented from seeing his father clearly; all he can see is the black bird of prey with the metallic beak.

As he sits in the boat in a very manly position with the tiller in his hand, he tries to trace his hatred back to its source. He gradually remembers his mother and the occasion on which she was hurt by his father's aggressive intolerance. He comes to see that his hatred of his father derives in part from the fact that on this occasion he was left as a little boy sitting by himself ridiculous and impotent, and from the fact that he was jealous of his father and afraid of him. The memories allow him to separate out and clarify his feelings and to reduce their power over him. He can begin to see his father in a new light. His father is a sad old man. But he is also a man with many positive qualities with which James can begin to identify. He has already internalised his father's self-image as the heroic leader of a polar expedition; James now sees that in this image there are two sets of footprints, his own and his father's. He shares his father's severe sense of uncompromising realism, staring death and loneliness in the face unflinching. Like his father he begins to dramatise this in a performance of some heroic verse – 'We are driving before a gale – we must sink'. He can now allow himself to be proud that he shares his father's estimation of life, of 'that loneliness which was for both of them the truth about things'. When his father praises him, he pretends, just like his father had been shown doing in Part I, to be indifferent to the praise as if it were not manly to care for such things. The lighthouse itself confirms for him some obscure feeling about his own character, for it is 'a stark tower on a bare rock', which provides him with a subtle and unconscious body image to match his severity and strength and to which his father's tall, lean and straight body significantly conforms.

This process of forming a stable identity and sense of self-worth is shown in *To the Lighthouse* to be particularly hard for a woman. The model of identity that is proposed for women, and which is perfectly exemplified in Mrs Ramsay, is to be always willing to sacrifice their own self in the interests of others. For example, Mrs Ramsay postpones her desire to work for the poor and the sick and to take up the battle for decent hospitals and sanitation until her children are grown up (which as it happens is too late). Moreover, the psychological consequences of this model of womanhood can be disastrous, because the rule which says always take other people's interests more seriously than your own may suggest that their lives are in fact worth more than your own. Therefore, self-sacrifice can destroy a sense of self-worth. Even Mrs Ramsay, who is universally adored for her womanly qualities, can wonder secretly, 'What have I done with my life?', having at least temporarily no sense of substantial achievement.

Lily is contrasted with Mrs Ramsay on the one hand and with Charles Tansley on the other. He is the very personification of self-assertiveness. As he walks with Mrs Ramsay to the town he talks endlessly and only about himself. Over dinner he annoys Lily with the egotism of his self-centred conversation. Lily herself is torn between different possibilities. She adores Mrs Ramsay but wants to preserve herself from love and marriage. She wants to take her painting seriously though she has a limited sense of its value and would be content to have it hidden away in attics. The problem of identity is posed for Lily in the question of how it is possible to be a woman without being like Mrs Ramsay. In Part III she has developed a much clearer sense of her priorities and seems confident that she has made the right decisions about her life (she has not married Bankes as Mrs Ramsay wanted her to). She is though still prey to uncertainty about her womanliness, as when she is confronted by Mr Ramsay on the lawn making his demands for sympathy and she compares her own frigid inability to cope with him (she draws her skirts closer round her ankles to avoid getting wet) with the way that Mrs Ramsay would have responded. Her incapacity for self-surrender makes her feel like a dried-up old maid, with nothing of value to offer.

So identity is not something which we can take for granted. It is an accomplishment, something that people achieve against serious obstacles and only after a great deal of emotional effort and learning. It is not only women characters in *To the Lighthouse* who are vulnerable to crises of self-doubt of course. Mr Ramsay, who tends to dramatise himself in stereotype images of male heroes (either those from adventure stories or romantic images of brooding genius) which have little relation to reality, falls into moods of self-doubt, thinking that he has been a failure. His life has been built around the accommodation of family life into his life as an intellectual. But the family consumes his time and gives rise to endless problems about money. Would his work as a writer have been more successful if he had held on to the identity that he had as a solitary young man?

Mrs Ramsay's sense of self-worth is vulnerable to the silent gaze of Augustus Carmichael, not because he actually says anything but because he represents the permanent possibility that our lives and personalities may be looked at in a different perspective from that which gives us our self-confidence. Mrs Ramsay takes Carmichael's gaze to be a penetrating one which seeks out her hidden selfishness beneath the surface performance of her self-sacrificing services to others. There is no interpretation of a life which is immune to this kind of challenge, which could be certain that there is no hidden meaning which, suddenly appearing on the surface, would fragment the delicate tissue of identity. This is because the construction of self is always an unfinished business. It is one of the ways in which *To the*

Lighthouse is a modern novel that it takes the question of self to be permanently open. Traditional novels often ended with a self established, triumphant and indestructible at last. In contrast, *To The Lighthouse* suggests that even the most accomplished selves, those for whom there seems to be no more room left for doubt as to who they are or in what their worth resides, are built on insecure foundations.

Bereavement

When people die in *To the Lighthouse* it is always a brutal intrusion of non-sense into the lives of the living. They die because the framework of human time, the way that people have of making sense of their past in order to create for themselves a future, collides with some alien, non-human time framework. This occurs through illness (Mrs Ramsay and Prue) or accident (the shipwrecked fishermen). Even the war, in which Andrew Ramsay is killed, which is a social and not a natural event, is presented in the novel as a distant, unintelligible destructive force. In other words, there is in *To the Lighthouse* no religious or social vision which could make sense of death, which could give to people's dying an uplifting or consoling interpretation and which could ease the grief of the survivors.

Traditional representations of grief have concentrated on the shattering intensity of the emotion. *To the Lighthouse* paints a much more complicated and subtle picture. Virginia Woolf, of course, does not represent these processes using the language of psychology. She aims to capture their quality as subjective experiences by finding images with which to express them. The power of her depiction of these inner experiences derives largely from her brilliance with metaphor – the rope which immobilises James, the mutilated mackerel and so on.

She chooses the device of showing the characters all on one day many years after Mrs Ramsay's death as if she were less interested in the immediate shock of someone's death (we are given a brief glimpse of Mr Ramsay stumbling along a passage) than in the longer-term effects of the loss. It is as if it were only after a very long time that the characters are finally ready to let Mrs Ramsay go (we know that this was true in Virginia Woolf's own case, in relation to her mother). On this day, each of them performs a private ceremony of farewell which allows Mrs Ramsay to fade away. For Mr Ramsay, of course, the ceremony is the trip to the lighthouse and he conducts it very much as a ceremony, with readings and intonations of verse and ritual gestures (as though he were conducting a symphony, the children notice). At the end he looks back at the island, silently staring 'at the frail blue shape which seemed like the vapour of something that had burned itself away', as at the remaining mist of incense at the end of a service, or of course at the vanishing ghost of his wife with whom he has finally settled his accounts so that he can now leap as if released or rejuvenated onto the rock.

The basic metaphor here is that of distance, on which, as Lily notes, everything depends. In order to be able to say farewell to the dead one must first get them into perspective. If one remains too close to them then everything becomes confused, mixed up together. It is as if, for proper mourning, we need to be as long-sighted as Mr Ramsay, for only as the distance increases does the dead person come clearly into focus. This is clearest in the case of James in whom there is a very powerful muddle of emotions, in which hatred and resentment are mixed with jealously, anger, love and admiration. His feelings about his father can only be resolved, clearly discriminated and assigned to their proper place when, after so many years, he can trace them back to the scenes in his childhood when he was overwhelmed by them. Although it is not spelled out explicitly we can perceive the outlines of some process of clarification taking place in his mind in relation to his mother. In particular he separates out his anger at his father's tyranny from his anger at his mother's disappearance.

This problem of gaining sufficient distance from someone in order to be able to perceive them clearly, is particularly severe for a child in relation to its parents. A child tends to attribute all sorts of magic powers to its parents, as does James to both his father, whom he sees as a monstrous bird and to his mother whom he associates with the magical yellow eye of the lighthouse. Lily has the same problem with Mrs Ramsay, who is a mother-figure for her. Mrs Ramsay is deified, or perceived as an angel, by many of those around her. But Lily goes further than this (in Part I) for she thinks that Mrs Ramsay has some secret knowledge hidden in her heart, 'like the treasures in the tombs of kings, tablets bearing sacred inscriptions, which if one could spell them out would teach one everything'. This is a typical infantile fantasy which children have about their parents or about other adults. You are grown up, it has been said, when you realise that there are no more secrets being hidden from you, no more hidden places like Mrs Ramsay's heart for you to penetrate. Therefore, the loss of parents or other idealised figures feels especially irreparable, for with them one loses magical protective powers and is left unsafe in the world. Both James and Lily have to learn to see Mrs Ramsay as a woman, with all the limitations and contradictions and negative aspects that this implies before they can really accept that her death is a fact and not some hostile withdrawal.

The passage of time accomplishes this work for, as Lily notes, after a time the dead do begin to seem dated and dusty. The perspective which they had on things inevitably becomes less and less satisfactory as life moves on. We come increasingly to have patronising feelings of superiority to them. For example, the Rayleys' marriage turns out not to be a success and Lily can feel that this vindicates her view as against Mrs Ramsay's about marriage. The simple passage of time undoes the authority of the dead and unmasks them as limited, mistaken, flawed human beings after all. Moreover, social conventions change so that those which the dead personified when they were alive become old-fashioned or even perceived as positively oppressive and dehumanising. Conventional women's roles, for example, changed a great deal between Mrs Ramsay's and Lily's generations (and have, of course, changed even more subsequently) so that it is almost impossible not to see Mrs Ramsay (and so many fictional Victorian women) as hopelessly trapped in degrading and oppressive roles and relationships. This inevitably means that we are tempted to see them as having limited vision and social understanding. It is very hard to have a fair view of the dead. This can enter into the process of mourning as a mechanism of release from the thrall in which they have held us while alive.

This is spelled out in most detail in the case of Lily Briscoe. As she paints her picture, her memories of Mrs Ramsay undergo a simplification and clarification, as though she were editing them in order to arrive at images which contained clearly a sense of her, whether sitting on the beach or sitting, knitting at the window. At the end of her day of mourning, Lily also enacts in her mind a ceremony of farewell. With her painter's very visual imagination she pictures Mrs Ramsay walking away across the fields clutching her flowers. In Lily's case also there are extra details of the process of mourning which are of general relevance. She, like James, feels anger, though with her it is more clearly directed at Mrs Ramsay herself. Also, early in the day she feels guilt at her absence of feeling, her indifference surprises her and makes her feel uncomfortable. Anger and guilty indifference are normal aspects of mourning. Perhaps what is most striking in Lily's case is that she experiences the sudden upsurges of grief as shocking and surprising. Grief is not a constant feeling but more like a dammed up volcano and it is a very physical feeling (what Lily calls an emotion of the body) which is especially painful, she feels, because there are no words in which it can be expressed (they always miss their target) so that we are left confused and feeling out of control (in the marvellous image, like being thrown wounded and bleeding into the sea). She learns that even episodes in one's life which one had felt were safely done with are not necessarily dealt with forever but can come back with quite shocking force. Emotional life, she learns, can be very disconcerting, full of shocks from the past from which there is no shelter and which can grab suddenly with quite disorienting force, like a hand rising up with a knife to slit through the fabric of one's composure.

3.2 MEN AND WOMEN

Watching Mr and Mrs Ramsay strolling together in the garden, Lily Briscoe finds that they seem to exist on another level. They are not just this particular couple, they are also a symbol. They signify the general idea of marriage. They can be at one and the same time this particular married couple, with all their individual quirks and particularities, and simultaneously an abstraction, 'marriage'. Lily looks at them and thinks, 'so that is marriage' and allows the scene to focus her mind on this aspect of marriage, that it is a comfortable union of effortless domestic harmony. It is typical that whenever concrete people or fictional characters are taken in this way to signify an abstract concept and to display its essence, this is liable to encourage oversimplification. For example, marriage as it is displayed at that one moment in the evening in the garden gives Lily a one-sided idea of it and indeed she knows well that marriage can also be something less harmonious, involving dominance, subservience and misunderstanding.

For the reader there are moments when the characters seem to exist on two different levels in this way. They are both many-sided, complex individuals and simultaneously they seem to stand in for or symbolise some general idea. Very often in *To the Lighthouse* they signify the general ideas of masculinity and femininity. For example, over and above the particular individuals Charles Tansley and Lily Briscoe, these two are also a contrasting pair who signify the masculine and the feminine. They stand in for and help to define the contrast between the genders. Of course, the fully complex male or female character, is always more complicated, more multidimensional than the abstract general ideas which they sometimes seem to be reduced to. There can be a conflict between the two levels, between the character and the stereotype to which they are expected to conform. Lily in particular tends to rebel against what is conventionally expected of her as a woman. Masculinity and femininity are presented as social roles and conventions which the various characters more or less comfortably and with more or less resistance internalise. They are not destinies in which people are trapped. In *To the Lighthouse* they are often made fun of. There is a large amount of affectionate mockery at the characters' expense, for the author seems often to regard them as willing victims of conventionalised expectations. The characters, like real men and women, can embody degrees of mixture of what are presented as masculine and feminine characteristics, and they combine them with many social roles and psychological attributes. The abstract categories like 'masculine' and 'feminine' are useful fictions which help us to illuminate the contrasting ways people live and relate to one another.

The opening pages of the novel rapidly delineate the masculinity of Mr Ramsay and the budding masculinity of his son. Virginia Woolf achieves this not through explicit assertion and argument (which is how it might have been done, for example, by George Eliot, with a narrator spelling the ideas out for us) but by description and images and ironic mimicry. For example, Mr Ramsay is lean as a knife, and we immediately learn to take this as a metaphor for the fact that he is wounding and insensitive (images of sharpness and cutting are associated with him throughout the book). He stands straight and strong and uncompromisingly faces the facts. Mr Ramsay's body is very expressive. His masculinity is always being performed in his postures and gestures. When he stands very straight and looks away into the distance, this betrays the self-flattering stories he tells himself about his explorations and journeys and leadership. These individual qualities of Mr Ramsay are elevated to the level of signifiers of his masculinity by being contrasted with the feminine qualities of his wife. Whereas he is uncompromising in his pursuit of the truth she tells stories, fantasises regardless of the facts, exaggerates. Whereas he is insensitive to other people's feelings, she is concerned and protective.

The picture of Mr Ramsay is comic not because his male values are laughable, nor because Virginia Woolf is unaware of the damage they do. It is comic because when the personification of these values in Mr Ramsay overrides his more delicate possibilities he becomes absurdly pompous and adopts theatrical postures of self-satisfaction (even though we know that he is in fact far from satisfied with himself). He makes a fool of himself.

The contrast between masculine and feminine in the case of Mr and Mrs Ramsay largely revolves around variation on two themes. First there is the theme of masculine egotism and inconsiderateness which is contrasted with feminine sensitivity and attentiveness to the needs of others. Secondly, there is a whole series of variations on the theme of masculine intelligence as against feminine imagination.

The first scene in the novel and the running narrative thread of Part I of the book is precisely this first contrast as it is exemplified in the differences between the Ramsay parents and their reactions to the idea of the trip to the lighthouse. Mrs Ramsay insists that the trip is possible in order to prevent James from being too disappointed. But his father insists that the weather will prevent the trip. He does this in a way that takes no notice whatever of his son's feelings. Mrs Ramsay is in general attuned to the needs of others, and particularly those of men, all of whom, it is said, she has under her protection. In spite of her dislike of Tansley, she takes him off on her walk so that he should not feel excluded. In general, she takes it to be her duty as a woman to make sure that the men are looked after and not neglected. This attentiveness is one of the main components of her duties as the creative hostess responsible for the success of the dinner party. It is a role in which she needs to call in the reinforcement of Lily Briscoe to help deal with the uncomfortable Tansley when it seems that the whole dinner might otherwise be spoiled. Lily protests and resists the social convention that says that as a woman it is her job to watch after the needs of Tansley. Nevertheless, she does in fact perform the role in order to help Mrs Ramsay. In Part III when she is faced with Mr Ramsay's demands for emotional sympathy, Lily feels that she does not have the capacity to respond as a real woman should, as Mrs Ramsay would have done. She is afraid that this failure to be what the conventions demand a woman should be means that she is all dried up, unlike the fountain-like Mrs Ramsay.

Mrs Ramsay's assiduous attention to her husband's needs is most dramatically seen when he comes to her demanding emotional sympathy and reassurance and she responds immediately by becoming like a breast from which he can, with his metallic beak, drink his fill of her life-giving energy, her 'delicious fecundity'. Here, as elsewhere, the contrast between the masculine and the feminine is not drawn explicitly but is developed through a series of images. Mrs Ramsay at her most womanly is the very opposite of dryness; she is described as 'a rain of energy', 'a column of spray', a 'fountain and spray of life'. She is an embodiment of fertility in contrast with her husband's barrenness, with 'the fatal sterility of the male'. The difference between them is that whereas Mrs Ramsay is a rain of energy her husband is like a hail storm. In his angry outburst at 'the folly of women's minds' he batters her like a 'pelt of jagged hail' and a 'drench of dirty water'.

The male egotism with which conventional female behaviour is contrasted is most explicit in the character of Charles Tansley. As he and Mrs Ramsay walk to town he talks endlessly of himself, of his career, his hopes and ambitions. There is no indication that it even occurs to him to talk with Mrs Ramsay about her own feelings or projects. At dinner that evening Lily observes and is repelled by his egotism, his desire to impress, and Mrs Ramsay observes that his talk is all a matter of 'I - I - I'. 'He was thinking of himself and the impression he was making.'

The second main contrast is between the masculine mind and the feminine mind and this has many variations. In discussing this it is important to remember that these contrasts are being presented by Virginia Woolf at least partly ironically and not at all as a simple statement of fact about essential differences between men and women. One version of the contrast is that between the abstract thinking of Mr Ramsay on the one hand and the concrete, sensuous perception of Lily the painter on the other. Whereas the natural home of Mr Ramsay's intelligence is among concepts of the highest level of abstraction, Lily's mind is more at ease with the detailed colours and shapes of the surrounding concrete scene. When she tries to imagine his intellectual work she can only come up with a picture of a kitchen table:

> And with a painful effort of concentration, she focused her mind, not upon the silver-bossed bark of the tree, or upon its fish-shaped leaves, but upon a phantom kitchen table . . . which stuck there, its four legs in the air. Naturally, if one's days were passed in this seeing of angular essences, this reducing of lovely evenings, with all their flamingo clouds and blue and silver to a white deal four-legged table (and it was a mark of the finest minds so to do), naturally one could not be judged like an ordinary person. (26)

The comment about it being a mark of the finest minds that they should focus on abstract concepts rather than concrete scenes is an author's irony, mimicking and making fun of Lily's exaggarated respect for the philosopher and her tendency to think in stereotypes. Lily does this again when she warmly remembers how Mr Ramsay came down in two coats and had his hair trimmed into a basin – these are stereotype images of the absent-minded and unworldly intellectual.

The contrast is sometimes presented as being between masculine reason as against feminine imagination. Mr Ramsay obviously prides himself on his rational intelligence and his image for this activity of the mind is the very orderly, unidimensional journey, on which his thought moves methodically, step by step, from a starting point to a conclusion, from A to, he hopes R and beyond. Mrs Ramsay on the other hand is a story teller (she tells stories to both James and Cam). Her concern for the lighthouse keeper is driven by strong imagination of what it must be like to live his life.

This contrast is signalled early in the book in an episode which is a strong echo of Dickens's *Hard Times* in which the difference between the negative, inhuman rationality of 'facts' is contrasted with the warmth and excitement of the imagination. This is the central theme of Dickens's novel and is summed up in the difference between the harsh regime of the brutal factory and school as against the fun of the circus. As Mrs Ramsay and Tansley walk into town they see a man pasting up a huge poster for a circus, with bright colours and animals. Mrs Ramsay is immediately filled with a childlike excitement at the idea of going to the circus. Tansley, who has never been to one, feels no such excitement. Ironically his excitement is saved for a performance which is just as much a matter of colour, splendour and costumes but which is associated not with imagination but with academic success and the solemn celebration of the masculine mind. For as they come upon the poster he has been fantasising about a rather circus-like irrational performance, about how he would like to be admired by Mrs Ramsay wearing his academic robes, his gown and hood, in a procession. For the man, dressing up in robes is associated with self-flattering advancement; for the woman, it is associated with children's innocent entertainment. The irony lies in that Mr Ramsay and his disciple Tansley have been clearly identified with the idea of the superiority of facts over the imagination and fantasy. Mr Ramsay's irritation at his wife's insisting on keeping her son's hopes of a trip to the lighthouse alive is based on the notion that this is to fantasise, to fly in the face of the facts, and that facts are something with which there should be no compromise. Tansley though has himself been caught out by the narrator fantasising about himself and his own career in a way which is just as much a matter of wishful thinking as were Mrs Ramsay's hopes for the morrow's weather. The masculine commitment to unadulterated facts and intolerance for fantasy are shown to be based on self-deception. Mr Ramsay himself also indulges in fantasy and again it is of a self-flattering variety, when he imagines himself to be the leader of an expedition, or a hero leading the charge of the Light Brigade.

This is not the only time when the narrator arranges to have the men shown up as self-deceiving in their attachment to certain masculine values. For example, Tansley prides himself on his refusal of insincerity (and this could be seen as a particular variation on the theme of uncompromising attachment to facts). He senses the insincerity of small talk at the dinner table and will have none of it.

He is even quite rude in his refusal to join in. A little later, Lily, responding to the desperate plea for help from Mrs Ramsay, is pleasant to Tansley and tries to draw him into the conversation. She herself is immediately aware of the insincerity of her friendliness but she knows that the function of convention is that it helps put men at their ease. Relations between men and women are, she decides, inevitably insincere. Meanwhile Tansley, who only a moment earlier had been scornful of the insincerity of dinner table conversation, now happily allows himself to be drawn into the stream of the conversation.

The differences between and relative strengths of the masculine and the feminine minds are most strikingly depicted in a series of images. Mrs Ramsay, hearing her husband talking about mathematics, thinks of the 'admirable fabric of the masculine intelligence, which ran up and down, crossed this way and that, like iron girders spanning the swaying fabric, upholding the world'. (98) This metaphor is Mrs Ramsay's and shows the exaggarated respect for masculine thought which she trusts absolutely. (This is itself in contrast with the men, for their attitude to what they see as the workings of the feminine mind ranges from irritation to contempt.)

The author has wittily arranged for these contrasts to be caught in the differences in the Ramsays' eyesight. Mr Ramsay, who is said to be like an eagle because he flies so high above things and gains a broad panoramic view of them, cannot see things that are under his nose like the flowers. Mrs Ramsay by contrast is shortsighted and has a clear view of the concrete detail of things up close. The image for Mrs Ramsay's mind is that of an underwater observer like a fish. ' . . . at the moment her eyes were so clear that they seemed to go round the table unveiling each of these people, and their thoughts and their feelings, without effort like a light stealing underwater so that its ripples and the reeds in it and the minnows balancing themselves, and the sudden silent trout are all lit up hanging, trembling.' (98) The contrasting images of the fish and the bird are to be found at several places in the novel, as for example when Lily in her grief is compared to a mutilated mackerel thrown in the sea, whereas Mr Ramsay is said to be a seabird on a stake surveying the channel in the water. Whereas the female fish catches everything in a whole vision, the male bird is like a marker which draws clear distinctions and maps out space. The most obvious image for this sort of activity is that of the lighthouse itself. When associated with Mrs Ramsay the lighthouse is a yellow eye reaching across space with its caressing beam. When associated with Mr Ramsay it is a tower, tall, lean, erect, surveying and marking out space from its position of lonely eminence.

It is this metaphor of the lighthouse as representing the lonely guardianship of the male mind with which James comes to identify as they near the end of their trip to the lighthouse. In fact for James, of course, the whole novel represents a journey from the infant's association with his mother (playing with pictures and listening to fairy stories) to his young man's identification with his father. James and Cam both represent miniature and not fully formed versions of the adult contrasts. In the bedroom scene in Part I the difference between them is focused on the boar's skull. The budding masculinity of James is happy to confront this emblem of death whereas the young girl prefers it to be covered over by her mother while she is comforted by stories of birds and animals and pastoral bliss. In the boat in Part III we find that their contrasts run along lines which repeat those of their parents. Cam feels safe with her father. She likes to relax under the protection of men. She immerses her hand under the water and in her imagination she has an under-water, fish's eye view of things: 'her mind made the green swirls and streaks into patterns and, numbed and shrouded, wandered in imagination in that underworld of waters where the pearls stuck in clusters to white sprays, where in the green light a change came over one's entire mind' (169).

3.3 CREATIVITY

Many of the characters in *To the Lighthouse* are creative. Mr Ramsay and Tansley are philosophers, Lily Briscoe is a painter, William Bankes is a scientist and Augustus Carmichael is a poet. Each of them produces works which survive – poems, books, paintings, scientific theories. Creativity imposes order on things, constructs things which resist the inevitable destructiveness of time. Of course, just how long things survive varies greatly. Mr Ramsay worries a lot about his own works and wonders whether they will long survive him.

These high cultural forms of creative work are not the ones which are at the centre of *To the Lighthouse*. There are other kinds of creative effort which run counter to the destruction of the passage of time. The nurturing of children is traditionally a woman's role and it involves all a woman's creative skill and attention. All the paradoxes of creation and time are at work in Mrs Ramsay's relation to her children. She carefully raises them knowing that their childhood lives of security, contentment and enchantment that she helps to create for them cannot survive as they grow up. When someone destroys the beauty of Rose's fruit bowl, Mrs Ramsay immediately looks at her daughter Prue, for it is of her fragile, adolescent beauty and its vulnerability that she is reminded. As we later discover, both Prue and Andrew are to die young.

All creativity seems to aim at least in part to work against the destructiveness of natural, material processes, whether it is knitting a sock or raising a child. However, no amount of creative effort can guarantee success and survival. Domestic creativity, traditionally thought of as women's work within the division of labour within the family, is often concerned with spheres of creation in which the product has no more than a very temporary life before it is either consumed or damaged. For example, Mildred the cook spends three days producing her *boeuf en daube* for dinner. The dish is described in terms which encourage the reader to think of it as a work of art with its harmonious mixing of colours, textures, scents and tastes. However, it is, of course, created only to be immediately consumed.

In *To the Lighthouse* there are many examples of 'women's' work creating vital and beautiful things which do not last long. Mrs McNab, with her friend Mrs Bast and her son, rescue the house from falling into complete decay by their creative work. Rose creates a beautiful arrangement of the fruit bowl and Mrs Ramsay creates a dinner party. These forms of creativity are taken more seriously, explored with more respect, than has usually been the case in the novel. They do each produce something which is temporarily orderly and harmonious but they are things which do not have much power of physical survival. The beautiful arrangement of the fruit bowl is destroyed even before the evening is over, the house begins to become dirty and damaged again the moment the work of repair and cleaning stops and the mood of sociability and ease created at dinner begins to unravel as soon as people get up to leave. Nevertheless, each of these things is genuinely a work of beauty and pleasure produced by careful, focused and skilful effort and in this respect there is a similarity between these kinds of creative work and that involved in the culturally more highly regarded forms such as scientific and artistic work.

Mrs Ramsay with her rather morbid imagination is aware of the uneasy relation between creation and destruction. Her husband's endless worry about survival and fame and his cheerfulness in the face of the indifference of nature, suggest that at some level, in spite of his apparent clarity of mind, he lives with the illusion that time can be defeated, that by an extra effort of his magnificent masculine will, he could produce work of such extraordinary quality that time would have to admit defeat. It satisfies him that this has been achieved by Sir Walter Scott and by Shakespeare. But Mrs Ramsay, in her woman's world of endless creation-destruction, has no such illusions. The eating of a meal, in which the results of much creative labour are pleasurably destroyed, becomes for her a kind of emblem of the intermingling of creation and death. For example, when she realises that Paul Rayley and Minta Doyle have become engaged, she immediately thinks of the dinner as a celebration, a joyful festival honouring the creation of a new marriage. At the same time, she holds in mind a quite different meaning (and this may be connected with the tragic secret in her own past which she does not name to herself), of marriage as an emblem of human illusions, a futile effort to create something permanent, but in fact already infected, even before it is consummated, with death.

> And she peered into the dish, with it shiny walls and its confusion of savoury brown and yellow meats, and its bay leaves and its wine, and thought, This will celebrate the occasion – a curious sense rising in her, at once freakish and tender, of celebrating a festival, as if two emotions were called up in her, one profound – for what could be more serious than the love of man for woman, what more commanding, more impressive, bearing in its bosom the seeds of death; at the same time these lovers, these people entering into illusion glittering eyed, must be danced round with mockery, decorated with garlands. (93)

Mrs Ramsay's creation of the dinner party is described in terms which remind us of its analogy with a work of art. It is a matter of bringing together things which at the start have a tendency to separate or to stay apart. William Bankes, although he is seated next to Mrs Ramsay and has shown earlier in the day his tendency to be thrown into a rapture by her, at the start of the dinner feels nothing for her at all and is uncomfortable in this family gathering. Charles Tansley and Lily Briscoe are hostile to one another and both of them resist the social conventions which make smooth and pleasurable company possible. The newly engaged couple have come in late and are still upstairs dressing. Mrs Ramsay herself is feeling exhausted and unsure of herself. In order to bring things together and to make them smoothly function together she must find within herself the energy and will to work on all these resisting, separate people and to encourage them to create positive relations with each other.

As the dinner proceeds, her struggle against all the forces of resistance and apathy and fragmentation is narrated in terms very similar to those involved in the narration of the story of Lily's struggles with her painting. She has to overcome her weariness and then as the journey progresses she finds that there are passages of relative ease and relaxation and others when everything seems to be on the verge of disaster. In the end her efforts are successful and she feels that (though the dinner party itself will soon break up) she has created something that partakes of eternity, some moment immune from change: 'Of such moments, she thought, the thing is made that remains for ever after. This would remain.' (97) As she goes upstairs when the dinner is over, Mrs Ramsay thinks that she has created something that will survive in people's memory, something that because of its special stability and solemnity, they would come back to again and again. They would come back, therefore, also to her. This is her kind of fame and survival and it does console and please her: 'They would, she thought, . . . however long they lived, come back to this night; this moon; this wind; this house; and to her too. It flattered her, where she was most susceptible of flattery, to think how, wound about in their hearts, however long they lived she would be woven.' (105)

What Mrs Ramsay has succeeded in creating was what Virginia Woolf called a 'moment of being' or 'moment of vision'. She believed that these are moments of special significance which have the power to survive in memory and which seem to give us a particularly clear sense of other people and of our lives. They can reveal things to us which are normally covered over by the bustle and rush of active daily living. It is moments such as this which are the focus of the creativity both of Mrs Ramsay and of Lily Briscoe the artist.

Lily's art draws its inspiration from her memory of special moments and seeks to preserve some meaning or some sense of an illumination which they afford. As she paints, Lily remembers Mrs Ramsay and a particular scene does come to her mind with this kind of force, a scene which contains in a condensed and powerful way a strong and characteristic memory of Mrs Ramsay. It is a scene on the beach. Mrs Ramsay is writing letters, making remarks about some object floating on the water (which she cannot see clearly because of her short eyesight) and chatting with Charles Tansley. Lily herself makes the connection between the power of particular scenes in the memory and her art when she thinks of 'this scene on the beach . . . which survived, after all these years, complete, . . . and it stayed in the mind almost like a work of art' . (150) There is, Lily thinks, no great revelation which answers all our questions about the meaning of life. There are only moments of illumination like this one and it is with these that both she and Mrs Ramsay were concerned. Mrs Ramsay tried to create moments that would make life stand still, that would produce something permanent, 'as in another sphere Lily herself tried to make of the moment something permanent'. (151)

The creative process involved in Lily's painting is beautifully described in *To the Lighthouse*. Virginia Woolf tries to capture a particular state of mind that is involved in artistic work that is a seemingly paradoxical combination of intense concentration and freely floating attention. As she starts her painting (in Part III) Lily has to free herself from distractions and from the agitation that her confrontation with Mr Ramsay has caused. Starting the painting is a matter of taking a risk. It is to launch oneself into a process in which one allows oneself to lose control, to be swept along on waves of activity, rhythms of the body, the dancing of the brush. As she gradually works on the space on her canvas Lily becomes totally concentrated on the painting and yet at the same time there is a part of her mind that is loosened up and becomes full of freely associated playful images and memories, fantasies and connotations, that have nothing immediately to do with the subject of the painting and yet are mysteriously a part of the process. She is gradually making contact with hidden parts of her experience, deeper layers of her mind. This is very like Virginia Woolf's description of her own experience as she prepared to write this novel. She said that she slipped 'tranquilly off into the deep water of my own thoughts navigating the underworld' (Diary 14 June 1925). As in the novel, her metaphor for the creative vision is seeing under water. For Lily it is as if the process becomes spontaneous and she is drawn along by its rhythm. It is a rhythm 'dictated to her by what she saw' as she looked at the window and the hedge, but a rhythm which carries her along as though she were no longer quite in charge of the process. Her mind becomes a vacant space and 'kept throwing up from its depths, scenes, and names, and sayings, and memories and ideas, like a fountain spurting over that glaring, hideously difficult white space'. (149) The image of the fountain relates her creativity to that of Mrs Ramsay whose fountain of energy had been spent on creating not a work of art but reassurance in her husband.

Of course, artistic creativity is not only a matter of releasing material from the unconscious or of the ability to invest memories of special moments with condensed meaning. It is also and primarily a matter of creating form. The painting (or novel or poem) must have a firm organising framework so that it can contain and stabilise the mass of sensuous material (in Lily's wonderful image, it must be like the light of a butterfly's wing on the arches of a cathedral). It must, in other words, be composed into a whole. It is this that will allow it to perform that function that poems perform for the characters in *To the Lighthouse*. They provide such satisfaction because they seem to be able both to verbalise all sorts of important but subverbal experiences and to hold them together into a tightly organised unit. As Mrs Ramsay finds when she reads the Shakespeare sonnet, it was satisfying because 'all the odds and ends of the day stuck to this magnet; her mind felt swept, felt clean. And then there it was, suddenly entire shaped in her hands, beautiful and reasonable, clear and complete, the essence sucked out of life and held rounded here.' (111)

4 TECHNIQUES

4.1 NARRATOR AND CHARACTERS

The subject matter of *To the Lighthouse* is the subjective experience of the characters, the subtle shifts and turns of their mental lives. Since most of the narrative is taken up with relating these inner experiences, we might think that the narrative technique involved must be 'stream of consciousness' or 'interior monologue'. In fact it is neither of these, although it comes closer to being the former. Interior monologue is a way of representing the thoughts of characters in their own words as if they were speaking to themselves. There are some passages in *To the Lighthouse* which use this form of narration, but they never go on for very long without being interrupted by quite different kinds of narration. For example, the narration usually includes the explicit speech of a character, or their wordless feelings and sensations described in the words of a narrator. For example, when Mrs Ramsay is sitting reading James a story her thoughts wander off and she thinks about each of her children, and for a long time it seems as though the narrative is simply following her thoughts. But this is not so.

> She did not like it that Jasper should shoot birds; but it was only a stage; they all went through stages. Why, she asked, pressing her chin on James's head, should they grow up so fast? Why should they go to school? She would have liked always to have had a baby. She was happiest carrying one in her arms. Then people might say she was tyrannical, domineering, masterful, if they chose; she did not mind. (57)

In this passage there are two things to notice. First, the narration of Mrs Ramsay's thoughts is interrupted by narration of her external bodily actions (she presses her chin on James's head). Secondly, although the narration closely follows the stream of her thinking, it does not directly quote her own words. For example, it says, 'she would have liked. . . ' and not 'I would like. . . '. This technique of narration, which is called free indirect speech and which is extremely common throughout the novel, allows the narrator to render the character's flow of thoughts, sometimes in the character's own idiom, without making any attempt to produce the fractured and semi-wordless thinking that would most likely be involved. Our actual trains of thought are not in fact usually so smooth, so grammatically elegant and so continuous as the narration here depicts. This technique allows the narrator to produce a seamless discourse which can move with great fluency and subtlety from thoughts to actions and other external events, and to record the substance of the thoughts without the distraction of their actual form.

Much more of the narration is like a stream of consciousness in which the narration follows a character's consciousness through time relating in sequence all the thoughts, perceptions, feelings, memories and other images one after the other in the order in which they occur. However, these streams of narrated consciousness are themselves mixed with other sorts of narration. Sometimes the time stream that the narration has been following is interrupted in order to follow some connection back to an earlier episode. It is as if the stream goes underground to follow a hidden network of connections and meanings not because this is a realistic rendering of the movements of the character's consciousness but in order for the reader to be informed of the hidden, past experiences of the character that are needed in order to understand more deeply the significance of some present experience or thought. It is a technique that Virginia Woolf called 'tunnelling'. It is as if behind the present moment of consciousness there lies a vast system of caves and the narrator follows a route through some of these so that the reader is gradually more and more able to appreciate what stands beyond the surface and the open mouths of the caves where they come to the surface at any present moment.

Virginia Woolf's most notable and powerful narrative technique in *To the Lighthouse* is to create an ambiguity between the characters' and the narrator's voices. The reader very often cannot be sure whether it is the narrator or one of the characters who is responsible for the words in which the thoughts and emotions of the characters are expressed. In most traditional novels the reader usually has no trouble in distinguishing between the occasions when it is the narrator who is expressing judgements and making remarks and those when it is a character who is doing this. The narrator's voice and point of view are quite distinct. Look, for example, at the story which Mrs Ramsay is reading to James:

> Then he put on his trousers and ran away like a madman. . . But outside a great storm was raging and blowing so hard that he could scarcely keep his feet; houses and trees toppled over, the mountains trembled, rocks rolled into the sea, the sky was pitch black, and it thundered and lightened, and the sea came in with black waves as high as church towers and mountains, and all with white foam at the top. (59)

It is clearly the narrator who judges that the fisherman ran away like a madman. It is also the narrator who makes the comparison between the waves and church towers and mountains. It is not the fisherman or any other character who makes these judgements or who creates these figures of speech.

By contrast, we often cannot say in *To the Lighthouse* who it is that creates figures of speech or makes judgements, indulges in irony or affects a particular tone or expresses certain values. The voice seems to hover indeterminately between the narrator and the characters. For example, at the very beginning of the novel we are introduced to James's hatred of his father.

> Such were the extremes of emotion that Mr Ramsay excited in his children's breasts by his mere presence; standing, as now, lean as a knife, narrow as the blade of one, grinning sarcastically, not only with the pleasure of disillusioning his son and casting ridicule upon his wife, who was ten thousand times better in every way then he was (James thought), but also with some secret conceit at his own accuracy of judgement. (9)

We are told that it is James's thought that we are learning about here, but it is very unclear just how much we should attribute to him. The judgement that his mother is ten thousand times better than his father is unambiguously his, but is it James or the narrator who thinks that his father is enjoying some secret conceit, that his grin is sarcastic or that he is like the blade of a knife? On the one hand, such judgements and images seem far too sophisticated for a six-year-old boy and should therefore probably be attributed to the narrator. On the other hand, we learn later that James's relation with his father is full of Oedipal anxiety, that his father does seem to him to be threatening and cutting and sharp, that he is aggressive and a competitor for his mother's love. Therefore, the images in this passage do seem to express perfectly the meaning of James's hatred of his father and in that sense we might feel they should be attributed to him, that they should be taken as expressing James's non-verbal thoughts, as spelling out his unspoken understanding. In this case, we might say, the narrative voice is not so much speaking in its own right and with its own distinct point of view and opinions about Mr Ramsay, but rather that it is putting into words on James's behalf emotions and insights which he could not himself articulate.

In fact, these images seem to have a dual function. Over and above expressing James's feelings they also serve, by constant repetition and variation, to organise the contrasts and themes of the novel for the narrator, that is to say they serve a purpose which transcends that of any of the particular characters. Mr Ramsay is over and over again associated with images of metallic harshness (he is a knife blade, a beak of brass, an arid scimitar). These images contrast his selfish, demanding and threatening style, in short his sterility, with the submissive, nurturing, sympathetic fertility of his wife. They simultaneously express the thoughts and feelings of particular characters and, repeated in many different contexts, play a part in the ordering of the themes and issues which the novel explores.

It would be worth looking at another example of this narrative technique. Mrs Ramsay, sitting with James, suddenly notices the sound of the waves. Other sounds had ceased so that

> the monotonous fall of the waves on the beach, which for the most part beat a measured and soothing tattoo to her thoughts and seemed consolingly to repeat over and over again as she sat with the children the words of some old cradle song, murmured by nature, 'I am guarding you – I am your support', but at other times suddenly and unexpectedly . . . had no such kindly meaning, but like a ghostly roll of drums remorselessly beat the measure of life, made one think of the destruction of the island and its engulfment in the sea. (20)

This paragraph explains the moment of terror that Mrs Ramsay feels when she suddenly hears the sound of the waves. As before, it is left deliberately ambiguous to what extent this is a rendering of her explicit thoughts and to what extent it is a rendering of non-verbalised thoughts and images in her mind. There is also no explicit signal as to what extent these images are chosen by the narrator not only in order to describe Mrs Ramsay's state of mind but also to perform a broader function, to provide for them a thematic interpretation which relates her state of mind at this particular instant to the general images and themes of the novel, themes of impermanence, the passage of time and the power of water to express unconscious feelings and thoughts. The words 'seemed' and 'to her thoughts' do suggest that the analogy of the waves with the cradle song is one of which Mrs Ramsay is herself conscious. Notice, however, that it is 'one' and not 'her' who is reminded by the waves of the destruction of the island.

The destructiveness of the sea, and of nature generally, is a theme picked up by the narration in Part II of the novel. The thoughts narrated in that Part cannot be attributed to Mrs Ramsay for her death is recorded in section 3. In Part II the narration is lifted clear of all of the characters and seems to represent a non-human point of view and a non-human voice. In other words, when the 'narrator' does at last find a voice which is clearly not that of any of the characters but which exists separately and in its own right, then it is no longer possible to think of it as a 'narrator' at all, for this would be to personify a point of view which is non-personal.

We can summarise the significance of the ambiguity as to whose voice it is that we hear by saying that it enables the narration to perform a variety of different functions simultaneously. It makes possible the extremely smooth and subtle movement of the narration as it shifts between the representation of different kinds of subjective experience and between different layers of the mind. Gradually there is filled out Virginia Woolf's notion of what it is to be a human person. It is to present in speech to the world only a tiny amount of the huge wealth of images and thoughts which exist in the lake of our minds, material which sometimes rises to the surface from this great reservoir of images and meanings but which at other times lurks beneath the surface unexpressed, a great field of complex forces pressing on our minds from within. Her narrative technique is designed to dramatise the pressure on our experience from this large but hidden inner world. It also makes possible the gradual accumulation of condensed poetic meaning, as the images are repeated and varied and woven into an ever more complex texture which spans and contains each of the individual characters within one fabric of prose.

4.2 THE NOVEL AS POETRY

Virginia Woolf's novels have always been described as 'poetic', but it is not always clear just what this should be understood to mean. Sometimes it is merely a rather vague reference to the fact that her style, based on profusion of metaphor rather than accumulation of objective, factual detail, can seem to the reader quite decorative and aesthetically pleasing, rather like some of the craft objects or hand printed fabrics that were produced by her artist friends among the Bloomsbury Group. It suggests that what she aimed at in her writing was above all beauty of style. There are some parts of *To the Lighthouse* that are perhaps open to this charge, of being concerned with style at the expense of substance, with superficial effect rather than deeper meaning. 'Time Passes' has always been a controversial part of the novel for this reason. Some readers have felt ill at ease with its personified airs and draughts which creep around the house asking portentous questions ('How long would they endure?') or with lovely but lifeless sentences such as, 'So loveliness reigned and stillness, and together made the shape of loveliness itself, a form from which life had parted'. (120)

However there is more to Viriginia Woolf's poetic style than this and it is worth trying to define more carefully what it is. First of all, there is her use of imagery, which has already been mentioned above in connection with her narrative technique. Virginia Woolf's fluency with figures of speech was quite remarkable, as not only her novels but also her letters and diaries testify. Metaphors seem to have flowed effortlessly from her pen. In *To the Lighthouse* one use to which this talent was put was that the narrative expressed in richly figurative language the unverbalised inner world of thoughts, desires, fears, sensations and fantasies of the characters. Moreover, the images are worked together by repetition and variation into a tight fabric; they are not simply the author's spontaneous poetic effusions, but are a carefully crafted or fabricated piece of work.

In her characters, Virginia Woolf represents the way in which the inner world can become expressed or externalised by becoming associated with elements from the surrounding visual world. These can become invested with special meaning. James, sitting with his mother cutting out pictures from a catalogue, endows objects with the joy and bliss of his feeling of being with his mother. 'The wheelbarrow, the lawn-mower, the sound of poplar trees, leaves whistling before rain, rooks cawing, brooms knocking, dresses rustling – all these were so coloured and distinguished in his mind that he had already his private code, his secret language.' (9) Of course, James, a six-year-old boy, would not be able to spell out in so many words just what meanings were associated with these items in his private code. It is a code of visual images, emotions and fantasies, little private stories in which things have their place. When the characters scan their visual world, it is as if they are looking for things which they could incorporate into their private stories in this wordless processing that is endlessly going on in their minds. They hunt out elements in the landscape which conform to the shape of their inner worlds. In the novel, the written landscape is carefully crafted so that it serves this purpose for the various characters and thus comes to build up ever more complicated layers of different associations.

The process of assimilation of the natural landscape into the private symbolic worlds is just what the sonnet by Shakespeare that Mrs Ramsay reads is about (it is sonnet 98). A lover, missing his absent loved one, cannot appreciate the white of the lilies nor the deep vermilion of the rose, except as 'figures of delight', metaphors for the qualities in the absent loved one that he misses. 'Yet seem'd it winter still, and you away, As with your shadow I with these did play'. Similarly, the characters in *To the Lighthouse* play with things in their minds, turning them into figures for the secret, even unconscious, private narratives which preoccupy them. William Bankes, looking at the sand dunes, is reminded of the long walks in Westmorland which he used to take with Mr Ramsay when they were young men, and his mind throws up the extraordinary idea that their friendship is a mummified thing, long dead but beautifully preserved like the body of a young man with red lips buried in peat. This image, with its emphasis on the youth of the body and the redness of its lips, seems to invite interpretation. It seems to say more about the feelings that Bankes had for the athletic young Mr Ramsay than he himself knows or that we could ever confirm.

Similarly Mrs Ramsay, looking at the rooks flying among the trees outside her bedroom window, tells fanciful little stories about them – they are a family and the man, called Joseph, is fighting with his wife, whom she calls Mary. We are not told just what she herself consciously makes of the obvious associations here (with the Holy Family), only that she cannot herself describe accurately enough to please her the movements of their wings as they fly and fight together. The narrator tells us that as they fight their black wings beat out and cut the air into scimitar shapes. This description, which exists in the familiar, ambiguous border area between narrator and character, uses some of the same images as were used in the description of Mr and Mrs Ramsay when they circled round one another in their dance of demand and sympathy; Mr Ramsay was like a black bird which flies above his wife and roughly extracts the energy from her with his cutting metallic beak, the 'arid scimitar of the male'. Again the image is suggestive of a story from the inner world which is being expressed in a way which hides as much as it reveals.

Of course, each character, scanning the landscape for things which can be turned into figures and thereby made to conform to their own private world, brings to the task a quite different set of themes and issues, desires and fantasies. Therefore, when different characters alight upon one particular thing, each of them will make of it something entirely different. The obvious example of this is the lighthouse. The lighthouse is at the centre of the narrative in the novel not because it has some symbolic meaning which transcends all the characters but because it is a central and fascinating feature of their common landscape which has great symbolic potential, so that it can serve as a great variety of different figures of speech or figures of imagination.

For Mrs Ramsay, who plays with the lighthouse in her mind in the early evening when she is at last alone and the symbolic power of her mind is released and is allowed to play unobstructed by all the practical attachments and demands of her busy life, the lighthouse serves as a whole range of different figures in swift and startling progression. For 'one could not help attaching oneself to one thing especially of the things one saw'. (61) The lighthouse light becomes for her a kind of superego, an eye seaching out in her mind for any lie and dishonesty that might be there, and helps her to construct for herself a flattering image of vigilant purity. Again she muses on the power of imagination, released by solitude, to populate the world with one's own private meanings.

> It was odd, she thought, how if one was alone, one leant to things, inanimate things; trees, streams, flowers; felt they expressed one; felt they became one; felt they knew one, in a sense were one; felt an irrational tenderness thus (she looked at that long steady light) as for oneself. (61)

At this point there is released from deep inside herself an extraordinary image; 'there curled up off the floor of her mind, rose from the lake of one's being, a mist, a bride to meet her lover.' From being an eye the lighthouse beam changes to being a strange body, bent over her bed at night, and then to fingers which caress some sealed vessel in her, 'whose bursting would flood her with delight'. That the lighthouse has produced in Mrs Ramsay's mind this powerfully bodily, erotic imagery remains her secret. When Mr Ramsay a little while later tells her that he had seen her at that moment looking sad and wonders what she had been thinking, she flushes with embarrassment. 'No, they could not share that; they could not say that.' (65)

For the other characters the lighthouse serves in a variety of figurative ways. For James it is not the beam but the lighthouse itself, its erect height, 'stark and straight', which provides him with an image of his masculinity. His father, whose straight, lean body seems to encourage an identification with the lighthouse, stands alone looking out over the sea, a sentinel, thinking about how 'his own little light would shine . . . for a year or two'. (37)

Other features of the landscape also have this fertility, being turned into any number of different things. The waves, for example, are seen as a skin, as splinters of glass and as the mountains and valleys of a pastoral landscape. They are heard by Mrs Ramsay as both a child's lullaby and as a ghostly roll of drums. As James observes, the lighthouse is not just one thing; it is as many things as the imagination can make it. Since we cannot express ourselves, we can project ourselves out into the surrounding scene so that it becomes a mirror in which we can see ourselves displayed. In life this happens in fits and starts, in moments of heightened emotion or imaginative creativity. In the novel it happens systematically and in a way that is spelled out in words, displayed for us to see as it happens. This is why there is something magical about the fictional landscape. Perhaps the remembered landscape of our childhood years can also be magical like this, having been edited and reworked by our adult imagination into a world where things are ordered differently, more in conformity with our desires and our fears, than they are in the relatively banal world of our adult lives.

The fictional landscape is more powerfully invested with meaning than our normal environment. It seems to speak endlessly and effortlessly for the characters, not unlike the magical world of 'The Fisherman's Wife', the fairy story which Mrs Ramsay reads to her son. This is because, unlike in our world, there is an author who is using all her craft to provide in the fiction what is impossible in life, a voice and a fabricating, organising intelligence, which magically spells out the characters' inner lives for them.

The most audacious example of this power at work, of arranging for the world to speak out for the characters, is that point at which the figure of speech is no longer even grounded in an object to be found in the character's field of perception, but is as it were whisked into view by the omnipotent hand of the narrator from a distant place. As Lily breaks down in tears caused by the pain and disorientation of her grief, this God-like intelligence temporarily brings the fictional time to a halt in order to introduce an image; the image of a body, mutilated but alive, being thrown into the sea. (167)

The particular territory explored in this poetic writing is what Lily Briscoe calls 'the emotions of the body', emotions which seem in their intensity to live in our bodies like a physical presence but which we are powerless to express in words, for as Lily finds, 'the urgency of the moment always missed its mark. Words fluttered sideways and struck the object inches too low . . . For how could one express in words these emotions of the body? express that emptiness there? . . . It was one's body feeling, not one's mind.' (165)

The novel depicts the minds of the characters moving backwards and forwards between the literal and the symbolic ways of apprehending their world. The symbolic apprehension of the world, though it is vital and none of the characters lives without it, does not cancel out the literal. The world of fact, of nature, carries on unencumbered by human meanings in Part II of the novel. It is indifferent to the meanings projected onto it by its human inhabitants and its processes kill them (they kill Mrs Ramsay and Prue) with no concern at all for their human projects and aspirations. If the novel itself is symbolic, over and above the fact that it depicts the symbolic imagination of the characters at work, it is this theme of the presence of human meanings within natural time that it symbolises. The figurative material of the novel is so organised as to encourage the reader to reflect on certain themes and issues over and above the destinies of the particular characters. The landscape of the novel becomes suggestive of a certain way of thinking about life.

The most obvious indication of this is the repetition of the idea that life is a journey, and more specifically like a sea voyage, full of risks, and accidents and exposure to the furies of nature and requiring courage to go on. Sometimes this idea is introduced ironically, as when Mr Ramsay uses it as a self-glorifying image of his intellectual life. He thinks of himself setting out into the unknown to go from Q to R. 'Qualities that would have saved a ship's company exposed on a broiling sea with six biscuits and a flask of water – endurance and justice, foresight, devotion, skill, came to his help.' (36) The use of literary cliché in describing Mr Ramsay's view of himself, allows the narrator to indicate that Mr Ramsay is being made fun of and that we should not necessarily take his own estimate of his character too seriously. For example, to confront the facts of life and death without flinching or compromising takes courage and Mr Ramsay, thinking about his uncompromising truthfulness, tells himself a little story about a voyage by sea to 'that fabled land where our brightest hopes are extinguished [and] our frail barks flounder in darkness'. (10)

The setting of the story of *To the Lighthouse* and the central role in it of the boat trip across the bay allows the idea of sea journeys to be introduced quite naturally into the telling of the tale very frequently and in a great variety of contexts. In Part III the bay across which they sail has itself recently been the scene of terrible storms and shipwrecks, and Mr Ramsay chats with Macalister and intones a poem about it. Mrs Ramsay reads to James the story of the fisherman and his wife. All these 'realistic details' are taken up and incorporated into the thread of imagery which runs through the book and this returns the reader's mind to the idea that life is a dangerous journey calling for courage and full of hazards. Lily, thinking about marriage and its contradictions, remembers how the Ramsay family had to cope with the tempest of Mr Ramsay's angry outbursts. When he was angry doors would slam 'as if a gusty wind were blowing and people scudded about trying in a hasty way to fasten hatches and make things shipshape'. (183) At the beginning of the dinner party, Mrs Ramsay is weary and has to struggle to find the energy to begin 'all this business, as a sailor not without weariness sees the wind fill his sail and yet hardly wants to be off again and thinks how, had the ship sunk, he would have whirled round and round and found rest on the floor of the sea'. She turns to William Bankes and begins to blow life into the party and 'it was as if the ship had turned and the sun had struck its sails again'. (79)

To these many uses of the image of the journey are added those of the sea. The waves and their rhythm denote the unstoppable passage of time. Their destructive energy denotes the unthinking forces of nature. Sometimes people are described as immersed in water. This is a satisfying state for Mrs Ramsay at dinner as she surveys the party, suspended and calm. On other occasions it is a devastating shock as when Lily is violently overwhelmed by grief: she is said to 'step off her strip of board into the waters of annihilation'. (167) In 'Time Passes', as if nature were mirroring the distant horror of the war, the death of Andrew Ramsay and the agony and suffering of millions, 'there was the silent apparition of an ashen-coloured ship . . . there was a purplish stain upon the bland surface of the sea as if something had boiled and bled, invisibly, beneath'. (124)

These images return us to the question of the nature of the poetic writing in *To the Lighthouse*. They suggest that the text is itself not a bland decorative surface, a serene and pretty fabric of prose, beauty its own sake. The ghostly roll of the drums as the waves beat on the shore and the purplish stain on the surface of the sea recall for the reader the funereal theme of the book, that it is an elegy for the dead.

However, poetry is not just a matter of images. It also involves the use of language in a way which gives high priority to sound values. In this way also *To the Lighthouse* is a poetic novel, for the musical qualities of language such as rhythm, alliteration, repetition and metre play a very significant part in it. This is not necessarily consciously registered by the reader, though it certainly makes an important contribution to the experience of reading the book.

For example, the passage in which Mr Ramsay demands and receives his wife's sympathy is one of the most emotionally intense in the book. (38) The central images are of Mrs Ramsay as a fountain of energy, a breast at which Mr Ramsay satisfies himself, and of Mr Ramsay himself as a metallic beak which roughly stabs at his wife in order to get what he wants. There is a very strong sense of a physical interaction between the two of them and in particular of Mr Ramsay draining away his wife's energy. The words 'pulse' and 'throb' are used and repeated, and a whole series of metaphors of liquids and heat give an almost erotic quality to their interaction. Over and above all these images the description draws on the sound values of words to emphasise the meaning of the episode and to engage the reader's sense of the bodily excitement that is involved. For example, Mr Ramsay's emotional demands are described in words which convey with great clarity his rather brutal, insensitive thirst and the way in which he is perceived by his son as dangerous and threatening. He is like 'a beak of brass, barren and bare' and these words are repeated and varied so that there accumulates a subliminal sense of the alliteration and also of the stabbing and jabbing rhythm of his gestures. The sounds emphasise the cutting, metallic hardness of his thrusts and their repeated, mechanical urgency. Mrs Ramsay's strength is 'drunk and quenched by the beak of brass . . . which smote mercilessly again and again'. She is like a fruit tree into which 'the beak of brass . . . plunged and smote'. Again these phrases are distinguished by their insistent, forceful thrusting rhythm and by the suggestiveness of the sounds, especially of the **k** sound (in drunk, quenched and beak).

By contrast, Mrs Ramsay is described in this passage in words which emphasise by their sounds liquid (rather than metallic) substance and gentle, fluid rhythms (rather than short, stabbing gestures). The suggestion is of deeper breathing. Mrs Ramsay knows that her husband wanted to be 'warmed and soothed, to have his senses restored to him, his barrenness made fertile, and all the rooms of the house made full of life . . . they must be furnished, they must be filled with life.' The sound which becomes most noticeable here because of its repetition is that of the **f**. The relationship between man and wife is contained in the contrast between 'barren'/'bare' and 'fertile'/'life', which is distilled into the two sounds **b** and **f**.

The importance of word sounds in the novel is not unlike the sounds of the waves for Mrs Ramsay; it is always there as a significant background though it is not consciously listened to. Sometimes, however, when the sound is particularly insistent, we may become aware of it. For example, the reader might well be subliminally aware of the pattern of sounds, without being able to spell out its significance, in sentences such as this: ' . . . dazed and blinded, she bent her head as if to let the pelt of jagged hail, the drench of dirty water, bespatter her unrebuked'. (34) This is another episode in which Mrs Ramsay is a victim of her husband's brutality, and the words are like hail stones, stinging and unpleasant and coming down in waves upon her. As in a long poem in which sounds can be read in contrast with one another across large distances, these sounds are only fully appreciated when we come across an inverse image a little later. For whereas Mr Ramsay is here a downpour of dirty water, his wife as we have already seen, is a rain of energy, a column of spray, a fountain and spray of life. These contrasting images are consolidated by the contrasts of sound: 'drench of dirty water' is contrasted with 'drunk and quenched'; and Mrs Ramsay, instead of being 'dazed and blinded' has her energies 'fused into force'.

Or consider how the word 'stroke' is repeated five times in as many lines in the passage describing Mrs Ramsay's solitary contemplation of the lighthouse. The regular reappearance of the word 'stroke' mimics the hypnotic reappearance of the lighthouse beam and emphasises that Mrs Ramsay is falling under the spell of its rhythm. Her mind becomes receptive to the musical quality of words and the prose becomes almost song-like with its repeated phrases, 'sitting and looking', 'it will end' and 'it is enough'. In each of these cases and many more there is a very precise way in which Virginia Woolf's prose is poetic so that words become an accurate external equivalent to some of the wordless internal disturbances with which the characters are afflicted.

4.3 CHARACTERISATION

In her essay 'Mr Bennett and Mrs Brown' (published in volume 1 of her *Collected Essays*) Virginia Woolf argued that fictional characters are not simply realistic representations of people. They are fictional constructs and they are created according to certain conventions. These conventions differ from one historical period to another and from one fictional genre to another. What counts as a well constructed character is quite different in a historical drama by Shakespeare and in a historical novel, in a romance and in a novel of psychological realism. Sometimes the conventions have changed as authors have redefined their objectives or changed their priorities.

Virginia Woolf's own priorities were to use fiction to represent the subtle movements of the subjective life of her characters. She wanted to emphasise different aspects of what it is to be a person from those that were emphasised in much nineteenth-century fiction. She was interested in the tumultuous flow of everyday life and in the hidden, darker side of people's most intimate inner experience. She was convinced that the conventions which governed the construction of fictional character would have to be changed. There would need to be less emphasis than there had been on plotting the complicated external actions and lives of the characters and less emphasis on the details of the social context of their lives. The depiction of moral life, of the virtues and vices of the characters and their development, should no longer occupy the central place in the novel. These ways of creating character in fiction leave out what is most vital and individual in people and the forces which move and preoccupy them most intimately. For example, she believed in the crucial importance in people's lives of certain moments which remain in the memory (though perhaps not consciously) even though they are not necessarily dramatic moments or moments which people can themselves talk about explicitly.

Virginia Woolf developed certain ways of rendering character which were innovations at the time, though they have been used and developed by many other people subsequently. She developed the techniques for rendering subjective life which have already been discussed above. These techniques were firstly the verbalisation of the characters' non-verbal inner worlds, and secondly 'tunnelling' to accumulate information about their past. These each help her to build up the individual characters. In addition, each of the characters is described from multiple points of view, as they are perceived not only by themselves but also by the other characters. They are built up as a synthesis of different perspectives. As Lily notes, to do justice to Mrs Ramsay one would need fifty pairs of eyes and it is something along these lines that Virginia Woolf provides. No priority is given to the perspective on them of an omniscient narrator who tells the reader exactly what to think.

Finally, it is remarkable the extent to which Virginia Woolf avoids explicit psychological and moral vocabulary. The characters are almost entirely built up of anecdotes and images which depict their inner lives and not of judgements delivered in an objective language from an external perspective. There is remarkably little explanation of the characters' actions and choices. Why does Lily reject marriage? Why is Mr Ramsay preoccupied with fame? Why does James hate his father? In each case, rather than an explanatory account in psychological vocabulary we are given an account of the images in terms of which each of them experiences the world: Lily thinks of love as a scorching heat, Mr Ramsay thinks of fame in the stereotypes of masculine heroism, and for James his father is a black bird with a sharp beak.

As a consequence of these methods of characterisation, the reader is given less of an explicit definition or verbal summary of the characters than was usually the case in earlier novels. Although we arrive at a strong sense of their individual style of being, we are also aware that they are full of contradictions and are very hard to pin down in words. It is as Cam finds with her father, that as soon as one feels that one has grasped him as a character, 'he spread his wings, he floated off to settle out of your reach somewhere far away on some desolate stump'. (187) So even at the end of the book we sometimes cannot tell clearly what to believe about the characters and we have to do our own creative work to hold all the fragments and contradictory images together in a coherent picture, like Lily who finds that her impressions of Mr Ramsay dance up and down in her mind 'like a company of gnats, each separate, but all marvellously controlled in an invisible elastic net'. In some cases what seem to be crucial questions remain unanswered right to the end. Does Augustus Carmichael really not like Mrs Ramsay or is that just her nervous perception of him? Did Mrs Ramsay have some earlier, tragic love which caused her sadness or is that just ignorant gossip? The reader has not been told the story of the characters' lives.

Overall the author does seem to adopt a uniform tone in relation to her characters, and that is a tone of affectionate mockery, equal measures of fun and tenderness. Mr and Mrs Ramsay are both portrayed as admirable and lovable but also as laughable, affected, trapped in a web of Victorian sentimentalisms. Although we might feel that the women are portrayed more sympathetically than the men, they are all treated impartially with both respect and irony. There are perhaps two exceptions to this, among the minor characters, where the author seems to lose her patience and impartiality, and they are Charles Tansley and Mrs McNab. Her portrait of Tansley seems angry and full of snobbish sneers at his lack of social poise. It is as if Virginia Woolf felt it necessary to take her revenge on those who arrogantly affirm that 'women can't paint, women can't write'. Her portrait of Mrs McNab the cleaning woman seems cruel and unobservant. She is not credited with any intelligence at all and her ancient body is needlessly made fun of. In each of these cases it may be that Virginia Woolf is up against the barrier of class. Whereas her writing can cross the sexual barrier and she can produce sensitive and sympathetic portraits of men, she seems unable to cross the barrier that separates her from men and women of the working class.

Mr Ramsay

Mr Ramsay is a philosopher in his sixties. He is unsure of the value of his life's work. He has in his mind certain stereotypes from adventure books with which he likes to identify in fantasy. For example, he likes to think of his intellectual life as being like that of an intrepid explorer fearlessly marching on to his goal across inhospitable terrain. He is tormented because he seems in fact to have become stuck in his work; the journey from A to Z has got hopelessly bogged down at Q. He has in mind for himself the model of a Victorian sage like Thomas Carlyle. He assumes that this role legitimates the power over people which he exercises and the demands he makes on them. He is famous for his outbursts of rage in which he behaves utterly without consideration for other people's feelings, as when he says 'Damn you' to his wife or hurls his plate out of the window because he has found an earwig on it, terrifying his daughter Prue. He slams doors, he bullies his children, he is rude to his guests. In short, he is a tyrant. He is also ludicrously self-dramatising. He marches around reciting 'The Charge of the Light Brigade' to himself. He intones 'But I beneath a rougher sea, Was whelmed in deeper gulfs than he', on the assumption that his suffering is more intolerable and more important than anyone else's. He keeps his sense of failure to himself (and his wife) and affects a public indifference to praise or fame. He cannot, in a strikingly modern phrase, 'own his own emotions'. In short, he is a hypocrite and an egotist.

This negative account of Mr Ramsay, however, does not do justice to the complexity of his portrait in *To the Lighthouse*. Lily finds that he is venerable and laughable at the same time, and it is important not to lose sight of the fact than in spite of all his faults those around him do on occasions find him an admirable figure. He is loved and respected. Lily respects his unworldliness, his lack of concern for trifles. She admires his honesty and his intellectual autonomy. Bankes, Tansley and his wife all respect (reverence even in his wife's case) the unflinching tenacity with which he lays hold of the great questions of life and death. He confronts the truth of the human condition courageously (his wife suspects that it even makes him irrationally cheerful and gives him an opportunity for dramatic phrase-making). He is vigilant, a sentinel on the look out for humbug and deceit. He loves his children. He is devoted to his wife, admittedly in his own selfish way. With her he can be charming, even ceremoniously polite. His daughter observes that when he hands out sandwiches in the boat, he does so with the courtesy of a Spanish gentleman. Cam comes to feel great affection for him, without losing sight of his tyranny over her and her brother. He can be kind and considerate to her. He makes her feel safe. He has an easy and unaffected, unpatronising manner with the local fishermen. He is not a snob. His son longs for his approval and obtains it at last.

Mr Ramsay appears in many different bird-like forms. He is intellectually long sighted and has a panoramic view of things like an eagle. To James he is a black-winged bird of prey with a brass beak. He is a sea-gull on a desolate stake. He is a rook whose wings beat the air in the shape of a scimitar. To William Bankes he is like a mother hen surrounded by her chicks. In his own imagination he is like a hawk, fierce and unafraid. He is a many-sided character who, although overwhelmingly unlikeable, compels people to respect his positive points.

Mrs Ramsay

Mrs Ramsay is fifty years old and renowned for her beauty. Unlike her husband she is self-sacrificing. She expands her energy in serving others, her family, her guests and the poor. She is a willing victim of her husband's despotism. She suffers his extreme rudeness without protest and even seems to take it as confirming his superiority. She does not rebel against her subservience. She thinks other women could only find fulfilment in marriage. She is high-handed in her efforts to organise people into marriages. She is already even to her daughters a dated, old-fashioned figure and they are determined to do more with their lives than she has with hers, to find something else to do than take care of some man. Even to Lily Mrs Ramsay already seems, ten years after her death, dry and dusty, as though of another era. Although she can find men's egotism tiresome, she admires them and overestimates their wisdom and their capacity. She 'reverences' her husband. She is pleased to contemplate men's social power and likes to think of her son James as a future judge or high official. She enjoys the fact that men trust and worship women. She is comfortable with a definition of the relationship between men and women which is a compound of Victorian stereotypes of worship on one hand and reverence on the other.

She is thought by her family to be given to exaggeration and she has the role of story-teller to her children. However, although she is associated with fantasy and imagination (in contrast to her husband's obsession with facts) she has no illusions about life. She is pessimistic, even morbid. Her thoughts often turn to death, suffering and grief. She believes there is no reason, order or justice in life. Lyndall Gordon refers to her 'Victorian agnostic's sense of futility balanced by solicitude'. The word that is most often used of her is 'severe'. She has a streak of sadness, which may or may not be related to some tragedy earlier in her life.

Although she sometimes goes around in shabby or eccentric clothes, Mrs Ramsay is considered beautiful. When dressing for dinner she prepares her appearance carefully. She likes to be admired and hates it when she feels she is not liked. She makes efforts to win over those who do not at first like her, such as Tansley and Carmichael. She attempts to seduce them by being attentive to their needs. Although her life revolves around the logistics of household management, her style encourages men to think of her in less practical terms. William Bankes absurdly finds it incongruous to talk to such a woman on the telephone about the times of trains. He thinks of her as a goddess. In fact she is tense with repressed feelings. She has eight children, a demanding husband and a house filled with guests to look after and this can exhaust her and annoy her. She manages to maintain the outward serenity of an 'angel in the house' while secretly inside she can feel irritation and despair at the shabbiness of things. She is afraid to talk with her husband about this because of his inability to think rationally and calmly about money. She can temporarily feel secret outrage at her husband's insensitivity to other people's feelings. In other words, although Mrs Ramsay may superficially seem to be like the heroines of men's Victorian novels, endlessly patient and attentive but mindless, she is in fact far more complex and plausible than that. She is depicted like her husband as full of contradictions, though she is less mercilessly mocked than he is. Because she does not parade them as he does, her courage and endurance are taken more seriously.

The family laugh at her tendency to lecture the assembled company about hospitals and drains. In fact she seems to go about her charity work with seriousness and intelligence. Her work is not just a matter of comforting the poor and the sick with her angelic presence (as it might have been in a Dickens novel) for she also takes her notebook with her. She observes and prepares statistics. She makes a note of weaknesses of social provision and campaigns for their improvement. Being a Victorian wife, she does not have the space in her life to do this work professionally as a more modern woman might.

There is at the heart of Mrs Ramsay a central zone of closely guarded privacy, a 'wedge-shaped core of darkness, something invisible to others', to which she returns when the ties that keep her bound to others and to practical life are temporarily removed. This part of her is extremely deeply hidden from everyone else and she refuses to share it with her husband. When she can quietly sink down, as if into an underwater world, deeper feelings rise within her, feelings about which she is extremely reticent. The secrecy with which these feelings are withheld from everyone else may not be unconnected with the fact that they are associated with an erotic, ecstatic smoothing out of all her tensions.

James and Cam

These are the only two of the eight Ramsay children we encounter in any detail in the novel. In Part I James is six and Cam is one year older. James is described almost entirely in terms of his relationship to his father and mother. He hates his father and would like to kill him for he steals his mother's attention away. His impotent rage is beautifully caught in the vision of him abandoned by his mother, 'standing between her knees, very stiff' with his useless scissors in his hand. He hates the way his father teases his bare leg with a stick. He longs to go to the lighthouse which he sees as a yellow eye and associates with the magical world of fairy stories which his mother reads to him.

Cam is a wild child who rushes around and does not have James's quiet concentration. She is easily distracted from the little tasks her mother gives her. She is rude to William Bankes who would like to be a friend. Whereas James, like his parents, is described as severe, Cam is propelled by visions and fantasies. The contrast between them is displayed most clearly when their mother comes to see them in their bedroom. Cam cannot tolerate the boar's skull and has to be comforted by her mother's fairy tales, whereas James prefers to see the skull, not unlike his father staring courageously into the face of the facts.

In Part III of the novel, where they are adolescents, the attention is on their relationship with their father. They agree in finding him a bully and they have an understanding that they will resist his tyranny together. But they do not altogether trust one another. James can see that Cam is easily seduced by her father's attempts to show an interest in her. She feels approved of by him and safe with him. James's feelings for him are so dominated by his anger and hatred that he remains inflexibly miserable and feels that he is tied down by these feelings in a position of complete immobility. He slowly traces back his hatred and anger to their original source in a scene in his infancy. Only then does he become capable of a discriminating response to his father and allow himself to feel the admiration and identification with him he needs in order to grow up. Eventually he wins his father's praise for his handling of the boat and reaches an important turning point in his life.

Lily Briscoe

Lily is thirty years old in Part I. She is unmarried and lives with her father in London. She is still sometimes tempted by the idea of marriage and Mrs Ramsay tries to push her toward it. She is thrilled and made jealous by the engagement of Paul Rayley and Minta Doyle and longs to have a share in the excitements of love. At the same time she can find love a cruel and destructive emotion and she does not trust it. On this as on so many questions she is torn by conflicting emotions. Her identity is unsettled because of her uncertainty. Can one be a woman and not marry? Can one marry and still take one's art seriously? She loves the family life of the Ramsays and is persuaded that such a life would offer satisfaction. On the other hand, she could not bear to give up her painting and she likes to be alone. She longs for and also fears intimacy. She is tempted to fling herself in Mrs Ramsay's lap and confess her love for her but when they do one night have a talk Lily finds Mrs Ramsay overbearing. She feels 'violently two opposite things at the same time'. She is seen by William Bankes as sensible and ordinary and this is the appearance she chooses to show to the world. In relation to her painting, however, she manifests a tenacity and absorption to rival Mr Ramsay's.

By the time of Part III her identity is more resolved. She has remained unmarried and she does not regret it. She admires William Bankes and has remained friends with him but Mrs Ramsay's notion that she should marry has come to nothing. However, she can still suffer uncertainty as to whether she has not become a dried up old maid, no longer a real woman, as she does for example when confronted by the demanding Mr Ramsay on the lawn. She thinks of herself in very unflattering, modest terms – she is 'a spinster', 'a skimpy old maid, holding a paint brush on the lawn'. (167) Her attitude to her painting is equally modest. She does not expect any public recognition and thinks that her paintings will finish up rolled up in an attic. She seems to like to be inconspicuous. She is very glad that no-one hears her when she cries for Mrs Ramsay. She seems to have an over-developed sense of embarrassment and is liable to suffer feelings of inadequacy and insignificance. It may be, since Virginia Woolf wanted to use Lily as a figure through whom she could express some parts of her own self (her struggles over her identity as a woman and her experience as a creative artist) that she felt it would be unseemly for her to invest her with too much glamour, vitality or self-assurance.

5 SPECIMEN PASSAGE AND COMMENTARY

5.1 SPECIMEN PASSAGE

The passage is taken from the beginning of section 6 of Part I (pp 32-35). It begins with Mrs Ramsay remembering that her husband had blurted out 'Someone had blundered'. She is sitting with James.

But what had happened?

Someone had blundered.

Starting from her musing she gave meaning to words which she had held meaningless in her mind for a long stretch of time. 'Someone had blundered' – Fixing her short-sighted eyes upon her husband, who was now bearing down upon her, she gazed steadily until his closeness revealed to her (the jingle mated itself in her head) that something had happened, someone had blundered. But she could not for the life of her think what.

He shivered; he quivered. All his vanity, all his satisfaction in his own splendour, riding fell as a thunderbolt, fierce as a hawk at the head of his men through the valley of death, had been shattered, destroyed. Stormed at by shot and shell, boldly we rode and well, flashed through the valley of death, volleyed and thundered – straight into Lily Briscoe and William Bankes. He quivered; he shivered.

Not for the world would she have spoken to him, realising, from the familiar signs, his eyes averted, and some curious gathering together of his person, as if he wrapped himself about and needed privacy into which to regain his equilibrium, that he was outraged and anguished. She stroked James's head; she transferred to him what she felt for her husband, and, as she watched him chalk yellow the white dress shirt of a gentleman in the Army and Navy Stores catalogue, thought what a delight it would be to her should he turn out a great artist; and why should he not? He had a splendid forehead. Then, looking up, as her husband passed her once more, she was relieved to find that the ruin was veiled; domesticity triumphed; custom crooned its soothing rhythm, so that when stopping deliberately, as his turn came round again, at the window he bent quizzically and whimsically to tickle James's bare calf with a sprig of something, she twitted him for having dispatched 'that poor young man', Charles Tansley. Tansley had had to go in and write his dissertation, he said.

'James will have to write *his* dissertation one of these days,' he added ironically, flicking his sprig.

Hating his father, James brushed away the tickling spray with which in a manner peculiar to him, compound of severity and humour, he teased his youngest son's bare leg.

She was trying to get these tiresome stockings finished to send to Sorley's little boy to-morrow, said Mrs Ramsay.

There wasn't the slightest possible chance that they could go to the Lighthouse to-morrow, Mr Ramsay snapped out irascibly.

How did he know? she asked. The wind often changed.

The extraordinary irrationality of her remark, the folly of women's minds enraged him. He had ridden through the valley of death, been shattered and shivered; and now she flew in the face of facts, made his children hope what was utterly out of the question, in effect, told lies. He stamped his foot on the stone step. 'Damn you,' he said. But what had she said? Simply that it might be fine to-morrow. So it might.

Not with the barometer falling and the wind due west.

To pursue truth with such astonishing lack of consideration for other people's feelings, to rend the thin veils of civilisation so wantonly, so brutally, was to her so horrible an outrage of human decency that, without replying, dazed and blinded, she bent her head as if to let the pelt of jagged hail, the drench of dirty water, bespatter her unrebuked. There was nothing to be said.

He stood by her in silence. Very humbly, at length, he said that he would step over and ask the Coastguards if she liked.

There was nobody whom she reverenced as she reverenced him.

She was quite ready to take his word for it, she said. Only then they need not cut sandwiches – that was all. They came to her, naturally, since she was a woman, all day long with this and that; one wanting this, another that; the children were growing up; she often felt she was nothing but a sponge sopped full of human emotions. Then he said, Damn you. He said, It must rain. He said, It won't rain; and instantly a Heaven of security opened before her. There was nobody she reverenced more. She was not good enough to tie his shoe strings, she felt.

Already ashamed of that petulance, of that gesticulation of the hands when charging at the head of his troops, Mr Ramsay rather sheepishly prodded his son's bare legs once more, and then, as if he had her leave for it, with a movement which oddly reminded his wife of the great sea lion at the Zoo tumbling backwards after swallowing his fish and walloping off so that the water in the tank washes from side to side, he dived into the evening air which, already thinner, was taking the substance from leaves and hedges but, as if in return, restoring to roses and pinks a lustre which they had not had by day.

'Someone had blundered,' he said again, striding off, up and down the terrace.

5.2 COMMENTARY

At the end of section 4, it was related how Mr Ramsay, reciting Tennyson's 'Charge of the Light Brigade' to himself and allowing himself to get quite worked up with the fantasy of his being the leader of the troops charging to their doom, had suddenly bumped into Lily Briscoe and William Bankes, just as, unable to contain himself any longer, he blurted out 'Someone had blundered!'. The comedy derives from the fact that it is he himself who has blundered, breaking the rules of social decorum, embarrassing everybody with his self-indulgent exhibition of fantasy and inappropriate emotion.

Our passage opens with Mrs Ramsay, a few minutes later, remembering that something had gone wrong and with the phrase 'Someone had blundered' chiming in her mind like a jingle, but unable to recall for a moment just what had happened. The opening lines of the passage illustrate very well the difficulties we have throughout the novel in exactly locating the voice. 'But what had happened?' may seem like a direct quotation of a character's question until we notice the tense. A direct quotation of Mrs Ramsay's thought would read 'But what has happened?'. Similarly, the sentence 'But she could not for the life of her think what'. In direct quotation both the tense and the pronoun in this sentence would be different: 'But I cannot for the life of me think what'. Both sentences are in a style called 'Free Indirect Speech'. They convey what a character is thinking in a manner that suggests a narrator mimicking her thoughts. This second sentence sounds like one that would normally be spoken to somebody else and it is hard to imagine Mrs Ramsay giving herself the information that she cannot think what has happened in this way. The whole point of this sentence would normally be that it is the emphasis conveyed by spoken utterance which conveys the meaning. It is possible, though unlikely, that we are to imagine that it is part of a conversation that she is having with James who is sitting with her.

The next paragraph, starting with 'He shivered', is even harder to locate. The whole paragraph is too extravagant in its language to imagine that it corresponds exactly with what Mr Ramsay is thinking. Yet it is clearly his thoughts and feelings, his fantasy identification with the leader of the cavalry charge and the humiliating bathos of his encounter with Lily Briscoe and William Bankes, that are being reported. The paragraph gives a satirically exaggerated account of Mr Ramsay's thoughts in order to make fun of him, and it does so again in part by mimicking his own voice. The words which both open and close the paragraph, 'He shivered; he quivered' (reversed at the end), are a narrator's joke image for the humiliated Mr Ramsay as a frightened or wounded horse, and the formal symmetry of the paragraph, enclosed within these phrases to give it a kind of mock poetic mood, is another signal that we are encountering a story teller in comic mood rather than a direct report of Mr Ramsay's inner experience.

It is worth observing that this paragraph is formally equivalent to the paragraph in the previous section beginning and ending with the words, 'Never did anyone look so sad'. In this case the subject is Mrs Ramsay and the paragraph is a poetic evocation of Mrs Ramsay's mood in images which are clearly attributed to the narrator. They are as extravagant and romantic as the images for Mr Ramsay but are sympathetic rather than satirical in mood: a tear falls in bitter and black darkness into silent and motionless water.

In each of these two paragraphs we are a long way from psychological realism. They both rely on poetic symmetries and risk moving too far away from normal narrative prose for comfort, with their rather mannered poetic images and repetitions. In Mrs Ramsay's case the result is a moving depiction of her deep but unexplained sadness. In Mr Ramsay's case the result is a comic deflation of his fantastic pretensions and perhaps also those of Tennyson's poetry which is directly quoted: 'Stormed at by shot and shell, boldy we rode and well' and so on. More fun is added by the fact that Mr Ramsay imagines himself to be like a hawk, a noble bird of prey and very much a contrast to the flock of starlings which his son Jasper shoots at the very second when Mr Ramsay blurts out his doom-laden 'Someone had blundered'. We feel that the author is really enjoying herself making all these careful arrangements.

In the next paragraph, starting with 'Not for the world', we return to Mrs Ramsay's point of view and as so often throughout the novel we also return from the mock symbolic to the literal level of narrative. Mrs Ramsay realises that her husband is distressed. She transfers onto James the feeling of tenderness that this elicits. The triangle of relationships between the two parents and the son is a central theme of the novel. Mrs Ramsay's love is mobile and is easily displaced from father to son or vice versa. Here James is the recipient but a little later in the day his mother's love is removed from him when his father demands attention and James will still remember the fury this causes him ten years later.

Mr Ramsay, his equanimity restored, approaches them and jokingly flicks James on the leg with a stick. This stick, poking his vulnerable bare leg, is also caught up in James's imagination as a symbol of his father's aggression and is long remembered. It becomes transformed in James's anxious mind into a sharp instrument which could do him vital harm and images of knives and blades and cutting crowd his imagination. Ten years later, hating his father intensely, James remembers 'the beak on his bare legs where it had struck when he was a child' for the emotion associated with the incident becomes condensed into the image of his father as a metallic bird threatening to cut off his right to speak. It is a subtle and convincing depiction of castration anxiety.

We may notice towards the end of this paragraph once again a sense that the language is no longer straightforwardly literal. Sound values of words begin again to assume a certain weight. Although this may be subconsciously registered by the reader one does not usually stop to analyse just where the sensation is coming from. Here we might note 'custom crooning its soothing rhythm', which itself contains the repeated soothing **oo** sound as well as a witty reminder that Mr Ramsay the soldier hawk is now transformed into Mr Ramsay the familial dove. Mr Ramsay the father is associated with a striking string of words, which accumulatively convey his threatening manner in relation to James: 'tickle', 'bare calf', 'sprig', 'flicking his sprig', 'tickling spray' and 'teased'. It is hard to be precise about the effects of sound values but it does seem clear that some of these words must have been chosen for their sounds. It is perhaps only later, after they have been repeated and heightened in other scenes (especially in words like 'smote', 'struck', 'scimitar',) that they take on their full significance and we realise that this cluster of sounds, **s**, **t**, and **k** with variations such as **g** and additions such as **b** have become firmly associated with James's anxiety about his father.

The narration moves on to an exchange between **Mr and Mrs** Ramsay which shows their relationship at its worst. **Mrs Ramsay**, still wishing to protect her son from disappointment, is still talking in terms of the trip to the lighthouse being possible the next day. Her husband explodes in rage at her refusal to face the fact that the weather will not permit it. He curses her (notice the alliteration in 'He stamped his foot on the stone step'; the sounds are now firmly if subconsciously attached in the reader's mind to Mr Ramsay's harshness and aggression). Mr Ramsay is utterly without sensitivity to other people's feelings here and is extremely rude to his wife. She is outraged by his behaviour but instead of protesting she submits silently to his anger. She is a willing victim. As soon as her husband implicitly apologises by offering to ask the Coastguards, she allows herself to reverence him and to feel that his certainty, his uncompromising attachment to the truth, provides her with a kind of security. She seems to feel that the demands made on her all day reduce her to no more than a sponge full of emotions. She cannot function except by relating to people's needs and demands. Her husband provides her with something she cannot provide for herself which is judgement, attachment to objective reality. She feels that she is his inferior.

What is being powerfully and convincingly dramatised here is the way in which gender roles are reproduced between the sexes. The woman's role is to nurture and protect. The man's is to face reality, to exercise power and reestablish his position of superiority. Mr Ramsay is ashamed of his embarrassing indulgence with Tennyson's poem, but neither here nor later does he seem to feel ashamed of his behaviour to his wife and son. Mrs Ramsay represses the anger that she had briefly felt and allows herself to be defined in stereotyped fashion as typically irrational (for Mr Ramsay uses the incident not only to berate his wife but to confirm his belief in 'the folly of women's minds'). Thus are their masculine and feminine identities consolidated.

The paragraph which relates to Mrs Ramsay's submission to her husband's violence is another example of how at moments of heightened emotional tension the language of the narration itself becomes heightened and more poetic as if it can only do justice to the feelings of the characters by multiplying the imagery and the masculinity of the language. Mrs Ramsay performs with the gestures of her body her submission to her husband's will as she bends her head and allows herself to be punished in silence. She is 'dazed and blinded' by a 'pelt of jagged hail' and a 'drench of dirty water' which 'bespatter her unrebuked'. The image of a storm of dirty rain beautifully captures the force of Mr Ramsay's contempt. Perhaps the power of the image is only fully appreciated when it is contrasted with its opposite in the next section, the image of Mrs Ramsay selflessly providing comfort for her husband's battered ego, in the form of a 'rain of energy', a 'fountain and spray of life'.

Our passage concludes ironically with Mr Ramsay, who has just been infuriated by the alleged irrationality of women, returning to his walk on the terrace and his own irrational indulgence in schoolboy fantasy. His wife, affectionately in the circumstances, sees him as a great sea lion splashing about in his tank. The whole episode ends where it had begun with Mr Ramsay striding off muttering 'Someone had blundered'. This typical formal symmetry is like the end of a movement in a symphony when it returns briefly for a last statement of the musical theme, its tensions now resolved, equilibrium now restored.

6 CRITICAL RECEPTION

When Leonard Woolf read the manuscript of *To the Lighthouse* he pronounced it his wife's best work. It was in his view a psychological poem and a masterpiece. Virginia Woolf's sister, Vanessa Bell, naturally read it with their parents in mind. Her reaction was totally positive: 'It seems to me that in the first part of the book you have given a portrait of mother which is more like her to me than anything I could ever have conceived of as possible. It is almost painful to have her so raised from the dead . . . [It is] shattering to find oneself face to face with those two again.' (Vanessa Bell's letter is printed in an Appendix to volume 3 of Virginia Woolf's *Letters*.)

Her friends reacted to the book enthusiastically, though there were doubts and discussions, as there have been ever since, about the success of the audacious experiment in narrative technique in Part II of the book. Sales were modest, though they pleased the author for she was still thought of as a difficult writer and only known to a quite narrow audience. She recorded in her diary in May 1927, a few days before the publication of *To the Lighthouse*, that 'in spite of obscurity, affectation and so on, my sales rise steadily'. They had sold 1220 before publication which she thought 'for a writer like I am is not bad'. The sales climbed to 2000 over the months and although this pleased her it does indicate how she was still then read by very few people. Reviews were polite.

Over the next ten years her fame grew and she became established as an important writer with a steadily growing audience. Her reputation as a serious writer was such that books began to be written about her and her books were translated into foreign languages. By the end of her life in 1941, she was already seen by many as a rather dated writer, associated with the prettiness and aesthetic experimentation of the Bloomsbury Group and unable to write in a way appropriate for the years of the late thirties, years when issues about which her novels had had very little to say were at the top of the agenda. The rise of fascism, the Spanish Civil War, the Depression with its appalling levels of unemployment, and the threat of renewed European war, made this a very different world from that of the twenties. Perhaps in these years her focus on the minutiae of subjectivity and the lyricism of her style and the absence in her work of political or social analysis made her novels seem of limited relevance. Although it is true that her fame and her sales never ceased to grow in her lifetime, by 1941 when she died, with Europe at war and the rather decadent culture of the twenties seeming to be of another age, Virginia Woolf had an uncertain position in English letters.

E.M. Forster, who was a friend of Virginia Woolf's and himself a novelist (he wrote *A Passage to India* and *Howards End*, for example) saw her work as part of a rich harvest of new fiction in the first decades of the century which drew upon the development of what he called 'the new psychological movement' (see Forster's essay 'English Prose between 1918 and 1939' in *Two Cheers for Democracy*). Her writing, in other words, did not represent a totally individual move into the area of subjective experience and the unconscious, but was part of a more general cultural development. Other authors such as Dorothy Richardson, James Joyce, D.H. Lawrence and Elizabeth Bowen, were also developing ways of representing unconscious forces and fragmented personalities, partly of course under the influence of the writing of Sigmund Freud. Forster also believed, however, that some degeneration of our culture had occurred. Whereas previous generations had been familiar with the Bible and with Bunyan, works which had opened for them the world of serious literature, the mass of people now were without roots in this traditional literary culture. Consequently, he argued, any modern novelist had to choose between being crassly popular and being serious. For this reason the characteristic of the serious novels of the modern period is their 'esotericism'. This is the reason why Virginia Woolf is among the 'difficult' writers.

Forster was not alone in the thirties in believing that a gap had opened up between the literature read and enjoyed by the great majority of readers and that appreciated by the cultivated elite. In the nineteenth century there had not always been such a gap, as the obvious example of Dickens demonstrates. His novels first appeared in cheap weekly or monthly form with an immense readership of hundreds of thousands. Later they would appear in the standard three-volume cloth-bound edition for the more wealthy. Q.D. Leavis, in her book *Fiction and the Reading Public* (1932) argued along the same lines as Forster. She said that this wide audience for great literature had existed also in the eighteenth century and earlier and that writers such as Sterne and Bunyan were enjoyed by the mass of people and not only by a narrow elite. In the twentieth century a wide gulf had opened up between popular and serious fiction. It was in this context that the narrow appeal of Virginia Woolf was to be understood.

Virginia Woolf was deemed to be among the least easily readable even of the 'serious' writers, such as Forster, James Joyce and D.H. Lawrence. One of Q.D. Leavis's informants wrote: 'Virginia Woolf fascinates but irritates me, an effect I find she has on a good many readers. Her genius is, of course, undeniable.' This estimation of her work, that it was brilliant but not much of a pleasure to read, was a common one. Her novels lacked everything most people wanted in a novel; clearly defined characters, dramatic development and plot, clear moral analysis and a resolution of everything at the end.

Not only did her novels lack these desiderata, but they were also written in an unfamiliar idiom, one which it quickly became common to refer to as 'poetic'. It was argued by some that her talents were not novelistic at all and that the beauty of her writing would be better accommodated within some other form, some form in which she would be less required to provide what she obviously did not like, namely factual detail and social context. Q.D. Leavis's final estimation of *To the Lighthouse* was that it 'is not a popular novel (though it has already taken its place as a important one)', which was somewhat more positive, however grudgingly, than the verdict of her husband F.R. Leavis that *To the Lighthouse* was 'a decidedly minor affair' (cited in Morris Beja's *Casebook*, p.20; see Further Reading).

When *Fiction and the Reading Public* was republished in 1965 Leonard Woolf responded by calculating the total sales figures for his wife's novel to that date and found that it had, over those thirty-eight years, sold over a quarter of a million copies in Britain and the USA. By 1965 it was selling some 23,000 copies a year. These figures do not necessarily prove that the analysis of E.M. Forster and Q.D. Leavis had been wrong at the time. Certainly, however, something had changed.

After the war new perspectives on Virginia Woolf's work were gained in three ways. The first was that she was fully assimilated into the academic discussion of the 'modernist' movement. Looking back to the early decades of the century, critics and historians could now begin to appreciate just how dramatic had been the change in sensibility that had utterly transformed European culture in every department, from music to painting and from science to the novel.

Virginia Woolf quickly came to be classified as one of the major writers of the modernist novel. As the academic curriculum expanded to include the twentieth century, her work was increasingly discussed in books and specialist journals. It was no longer a question of whether her books could find a general audience but whether they had a place in the canon of recognised great works of literature. It quickly became generally agreed that *To the Lighthouse* does have such a place even though there were doubts about her other works. There is a useful review of the academic criticism on Virginia Woolf that had appeared up to 1962 in Jean Guiguet's *Virginia Woolf and her Works* which was the standard book about her for many years. In fact most critics, as Guiguet points out, were still at a bit of a loss with the modern novel and measured her worth by hopelessly outdated criteria and assumptions. There was at that time very little appreciation of the significance of the great innovations in fictional technique that she had created. It was as if critics were attempting to understand Cézanne on the assumption that he was trying to paint like Ingres.

The central question posed by Virginia Woolf's novels which was so often avoided was the question of technique. In what ways exactly do her novels differ from nineteenth-century novels and why? What is it that is *modern* about her writing? These are questions that are at the centre of one of the finest pieces of writing on *To the Lighthouse*, an essay written during the war and not published in English until 1953, Erich Auerbach's 'The Brown Stocking', which is in his monumental work *Mimesis: The Representation of Reality in Western Literature*. Auerbach was the first to go beyond the vague generalities that were then commonplace and according to which Virginia Woolf's technique consisted of 'interior monologue' or 'stream of consciousness'. He was the first to analyse in detail the peculiar position of the narrator in *To the Lighthouse*, the narrator who is only ambiguously distinct from the characters and who has none of the omniscience of nineteenth-century narrators. Moreover, he analysed the representation of consciousness from multiple perspectives and the importance for Virginia Woolf's characters of their past which is seen as a stratum of time the recovery of which can be triggered by insignificant events. These various devices enable Virginia Woolf to represent consciousness in unprecedented ways and with unprecedented accuracy, depth and subtlety. Auerbach promoted *To the Lighthouse* to a position of being representative of the modern period and this status of preeminence was perhaps the novel's finest hour in academic criticism.

The second major impetus to a renewed reception of Virginia Woolf's work was the enormous flood of publications about her life and about the lives and social history of her circle of friends. From the mid-seventies onwards Virginia Woolf's own papers have been edited and published, including her diaries, her letters, her memoirs and autobiographical sketches, and her essays. A biography of her written by her nephew Quentin Bell was published in 1972. Furthermore, there have also been a large number of biographies, memoirs and historical studies of her friends in the Bloomsbury Group. Because of the autobiographical nature of *To the Lighthouse* some of this material has had an impact on discussions of the novel. Perhaps the most important are her accounts of her memories of childhood holidays in Cornwall and her portraits of her parents, both in *Moments of Being*. There has been a tendency, more perhaps with Virginia Woolf than with any other writer, to assimilate writing about her fiction with writing about her own life. Typical recent examples of this are the books by Roger Poole and by Lyndall Gordon mentioned below.

The third major new impetus to Virginia Woolf studies has been the women's movement. Since the early seventies, with the renewal of feminism as an important current in British and American culture, there has been a very strong interest in Virginia Woolf not only as a woman writer but as one for whom questions of women's experience are absolutely central to her work. One result of this has been that some of her works which had begun to fade in interest are now very widely read, chief among them *A Room of One's Own*. Furthermore, certain questions are promoted to a place high on the agenda, especially questions about identity and its difficulties for women in our culture. Perhaps the best book on Virginia Woolf to appear as a result of this revived feminism is that by Phyllis Rose, *Woman of Letters: A Life of Virginia Woolf*.

In general the image of Virginia Woolf and her work has greatly changed over the last fifteen years, most significantly in that whereas previously the emphasis in discussion of her novels had been on them as poetic evocations of subjectivity and on her innovations in technique, one now often finds her treated as a writer who is concerned with social, and in a sense, political problems, namely the problems of power. We can now see that among her main interests are the power of men over women and of parents over children. In this context, portraits of Mr and Mrs Ramsay have a wider importance than simply as fictional portraits of the author's parents, or even as representing a typically Victorian relationship within a marriage. For their relationship raises questions which are still with us today, questions about emotionally crippled men and their aggressions; questions about the repressions, impotence and frustrations of women; questions about the way that these patterns of emotional life are reproduced through relationships within the family. The creativity of women, as represented by Lily Briscoe, and the obstacles to it, as discussed in *A Room of One's Own*, are also of strong interest to us today. Perhaps for these reasons among others, *To the Lighthouse* is read more widely today than ever before.

REVISION QUESTIONS

1. Hermione Lee says that Mr Ramsay is very largely a comic character. Do you agree?

2. 'The question the novel seems to have set itself is the one many women who read it must ask: How could Mrs Ramsay bear it?' (Jane Miller, *Women Writing About Men*). How could she?

3. Discuss the portrayal of relationships between parents and children in *To the Lighthouse*.

4. When Lily Briscoe watches the Ramsays she says to herself, 'So that is marriage'. Do we learn anything in general about marriage from *To the Lighthouse* or only about the Ramsays' particular relationship?

5. Lily Briscoe finds that relationships between men and women are extremely insincere. What does she have in mind and is she right about the relationships between men and women in the novel?

6. In what way does memory enter into the lives of the characters in *To the Lighthouse*?

7. What seems to you particularly interesting about the portrayal of artistic creation in *To the Lighthouse*?

8. Virginia Woolf said that she was interested in writing about the dark places of psychology. Discuss with careful attention to detailed examples how the narrative technique in *To the Lighthouse* enabled her to do that.

9. Illustrate what it means to say that in *To the Lighthouse* characters are constructed from multiple points of view.

10. Erich Auerbach says that the narrator of *To the Lighthouse* looks at the characters 'not with knowing but with doubting and questioning eyes'. Illustrate this.

11. Mrs Ramsay finds that a poem which satisfies her is 'a globed, compacted thing'. Could the same be said for *To the Lighthouse*?

12. Lyndall Gordon says that the narrative style of 'Time Passes' reflects the fact that 'war is a vacancy through which time rushes while home-makers and artists, the creators of civilisation, sleep.' Do you agree or would you emphasise some other explanation of Part II of the novel?

13. At the Ramsays Lily Briscoe feels violently two oppoiste things at the same time. Discuss some examples of this from *To the Lighthouse* both in Lily's case and in that of other characters.

14. In what sense is *To the Lighthouse* a poetic novel? Choose some passages and discuss their poetic features.

15. Does the idea of a collective stream of consciousness helpfully describe the narrative technique of *To the Lighthouse*?

FURTHER READING

The edition of *To the Lighthouse* to which I have given page references in this book is the paperback edition published by Granada in 1977.

Works by Virginia Woolf

A Room of One's Own (Granada, 1977). Originally published three years after *To the Lighthouse* this book is on women and writing. It is particularly relevant to the problems of women and artistic creativity portrayed in *To the Lighthouse*.

A Writer's Diary, ed. Leonard Woolf, Hogarth Press, 1953 (paperback published by Granada 1978). This book contains extracts from Virginia Woolf's diaries pertaining to her writing and there are many interesting entries relating to *To the Lighthouse*.

Moments of Being, Unpublished Autobiographical Writings ed. Jeanne Schulkind, Sussex University Press, 1976 (paperback published by Granada, 1978). The essay 'A Sketch of the Past' is particularly relevant to *To the Lighthouse*.

Biography

Quentin Bell, *Virginia Woolf, A Biography, 2 vols.*, Hogarth Press, 1972 (paperback published by Paladin Books, 1976).

Lyndall Gordon, *Virginia Woolf: A Writer's Life*, Oxford University Press, 1984.

Roger Poole, *The Unknown Virginia Woolf*, Cambridge University Press (paperback published by Harvester Press, 1982).

Criticism

Erich Auerbach, *Mimesis: The Representation of Reality in Western Literature*, Princeton University Press, 1953. Chapter 20, 'The Brown Stocking' is about *To the Lighthouse*.

ed. Morris Beja, *Virginia Woolf: To the Lighthouse: A Casebook*, Macmillan Casebook Series, 1970 (paperback). This collection includes early reviews, extracts from Virginia Woolf's diary, her essay 'Modern Fiction' as well as critical essays, including that of Auerbach mentioned above.

Jean Guiget, *Virginia Woolf and her Works*, Hogarth Press, 1965.

Hermione Lee, *The Novels of Virginia Woolf*, Methuen, 1977 (both hardback and paperback editions).

Phyllis Rose, *Woman of Letters: A Life of Virginia Woolf*, Routledge and Kegan Paul, 1978. This is an excellent feminist treatment of Virginia Woolf's life and works. Chapter 8 is on *To the Lighthouse*.

Mastering English Literature
Richard Gill

Mastering English Literature will help readers both to enjoy English Literature and to be successful in 'O' levels, 'A' levels and other public exams. It is an introduction to the study of poetry, novels and drama which helps the reader in four ways – by providing ways of approaching literature, by giving examples and practice exercises, by offering hints on how to write about literature, and by the author's own evident enthusiasm for the subject. With extracts from more than 200 texts, this is an enjoyable account of how to get the maximum satisfaction out of reading, whether it be for formal examinations or simply for pleasure.

Work Out English Literature ('A' level)
S.H. Burton

This book familiarises 'A' level English Literature candidates with every kind of test which they are likely to encounter. Suggested answers are worked out step by step and accompanied by full author's commentary. The book helps students to clarify their aims and establish techniques and standards so that they can make appropriate responses to similar questions when the examination pressures are on. It opens up fresh ways of looking at the full range of set texts, authors and critical judgements and motivates students to know more of these matters.

Also from Macmillan

CASEBOOK SERIES

The Macmillan *Casebook* series brings together the best of modern criticism with a selection of early reviews and comments. Each Casebook charts the development of opinion on a play, poem, or novel, or on a literary genre. from its first appearance to the present day.

GENERAL THEMES

COMEDY: DEVELOPMENTS IN CRITICISM
D. J. Palmer

DRAMA CRITICISM: DEVELOPMENTS SINCE IBSEN
A. J. Hinchliffe

THE ENGLISH NOVEL: DEVELOPMENTS IN CRITICISM SINCE HENRY JAMES
Stephen Hazell

THE LANGUAGE OF LITERATURE
N. Page

THE PASTORAL MODE
Bryan Loughrey

THE ROMANTIC IMAGINATION
J. S. Hill

TRAGEDY: DEVELOPMENTS IN CRITICISM
R. P. Draper

POETRY

WILLIAM BLAKE: SONGS OF INNOCENCE AND EXPERIENCE
Margaret Bottrall

BROWNING: MEN AND WOMEN AND OTHER POEMS
J. R. Watson

BYRON: CHILDE HAROLD'S PILGRIMAGE AND DON JUAN
John Jump

CHAUCER: THE CANTERBURY TALES
J. J. Anderson

COLERIDGE: THE ANCIENT MARINER AND OTHER POEMS
A. R. Jones and W. Tydeman

DONNE: SONGS AND SONETS
Julian Lovelock

T. S. ELIOT: FOUR QUARTETS
Bernard Bergonzi

T. S. ELIOT: PRUFROCK, GERONTION, ASH WEDNESDAY AND OTHER POEMS
B. C. Southam

T. S. ELIOT: THE WASTELAND
C. B. Cox and A. J. Hinchliffe

ELIZABETHAN POETRY: LYRICAL AND NARRATIVE
Gerald Hammond

THOMAS HARDY: POEMS
J. Gibson and T. Johnson

GERALD MANLEY HOPKINS: POEMS
Margaret Bottrall

KEATS: ODES
G. S. Fraser

KEATS: THE NARRATIVE POEMS
J. S. Hill

MARVELL: POEMS
Arthur Pollard

THE METAPHYSICAL POETS
Gerald Hammond

MILTON: PARADISE LOST
A. E. Dyson and Julian Lovelock

POETRY OF THE FIRST WORLD WAR
Dominic Hibberd

ALEXANDER POPE: THE RAPE OF THE LOCK
John Dixon Hunt

SHELLEY: SHORTER POEMS & LYRICS
Patrick Swinden

SPENSER: THE FAERIE QUEEN
Peter Bayley

TENNYSON: IN MEMORIAM
John Dixon Hunt

THIRTIES POETS: 'THE AUDEN GROUP'
Ronald Carter

WORDSWORTH: LYRICAL BALLADS
A. R. Jones and W. Tydeman

WORDSWORTH: THE PRELUDE
W. J. Harvey and R. Gravil

W. B. YEATS: POEMS 1919–1935
E. Cullingford

W. B. YEATS: LAST POEMS
Jon Stallworthy

THE NOVEL AND PROSE

JANE AUSTEN: EMMA
David Lodge

JANE AUSTEN: NORTHANGER ABBEY AND PERSUASION
B. C. Southam

JANE AUSTEN: SENSE AND SENSIBILITY, PRIDE AND PREJUDICE AND MANSFIELD PARK
B. C. Southam

CHARLOTTE BRONTË: JANE EYRE AND VILLETTE
Miriam Allott

EMILY BRONTË: WUTHERING HEIGHTS
Miriam Allott

BUNYAN: THE PILGRIM'S PROGRESS
R. Sharrock

CONRAD: HEART OF DARKNESS, NOSTROMO AND UNDER WESTERN EYES
C. B. Cox

CONRAD: THE SECRET AGENT
Ian Watt

CHARLES DICKENS: BLEAK HOUSE
A. E. Dyson

CHARLES DICKENS: DOMBEY AND SON AND LITTLE DORRITT
Alan Shelston

CHARLES DICKENS: HARD TIMES, GREAT EXPECTATIONS AND OUR MUTUAL FRIEND
N. Page

GEORGE ELIOT: MIDDLEMARCH
Patrick Swinden

GEORGE ELIOT: THE MILL ON THE FLOSS AND SILAS MARNER
R. P. Draper

HENRY FIELDING: TOM JONES
Neil Compton

E. M. FORSTER: A PASSAGE TO INDIA
Malcolm Bradbury

HARDY: THE TRAGIC NOVELS
R. P. Draper

HENRY JAMES: WASHINGTON SQUARE AND THE PORTRAIT OF A LADY
Alan Shelston

JAMES JOYCE: DUBLINERS AND A PORTRAIT OF THE ARTIST AS A YOUNG MAN
Morris Beja

D. H. LAWRENCE: THE RAINBOW AND WOMEN IN LOVE
Colin Clarke

D. H. LAWRENCE: SONS AND LOVERS
Gamini Salgado

SWIFT: GULLIVER'S TRAVELS
Richard Gravil

THACKERAY: VANITY FAIR
Arthur Pollard

TROLLOPE: THE BARSETSHIRE
NOVELS
T. Bareham

VIRGINIA WOOLF: TO THE
LIGHTHOUSE
Morris Beja

DRAMA

CONGREVE: COMEDIES
Patrick Lyons

T. S. ELIOT: PLAYS
Arnold P. Hinchliffe

JONSON: EVERY MAN IN HIS
HUMOUR AND THE ALCHEMIST
R. V. Holdsworth

JONSON: VOLPONE
J. A. Barish

MARLOWE: DR FAUSTUS
John Jump

MARLOWE: TAMBURLAINE,
EDWARD II AND THE JEW OF
MALTA
John Russell Brown

MEDIEVAL ENGLISH DRAMA
Peter Happé

O'CASEY: JUNO AND THE
PAYCOCK, THE PLOUGH AND THE
STARS AND THE SHADOW OF A
GUNMAN
R. Ayling

JOHN OSBORNE: LOOK BACK IN
ANGER
John Russell Taylor

WEBSTER: THE WHITE DEVIL AND
THE DUCHESS OF MALFI
R. V. Holdsworth

WILDE: COMEDIES
W. Tydeman

SHAKESPEARE

SHAKESPEARE: ANTONY AND
CLEOPATRA
John Russell Brown

SHAKESPEARE: CORIOLANUS
B. A. Brockman

SHAKESPEARE: HAMLET
John Jump

SHAKESPEARE: HENRY IV PARTS
I AND II
G. K. Hunter

SHAKESPEARE: HENRY V
Michael Quinn

SHAKESPEARE: JULIUS CAESAR
Peter Ure

SHAKESPEARE: KING LEAR
Frank Kermode

SHAKESPEARE: MACBETH
John Wain

SHAKESPEARE: MEASURE FOR
MEASURE
G. K. Stead

SHAKESPEARE: THE MERCHANT
OF VENICE
John Wilders

SHAKESPEARE: A MIDSUMMER
NIGHT'S DREAM
A. W. Price

SHAKESPEARE: MUCH ADO
ABOUT NOTHING AND AS YOU
LIKE IT
John Russell Brown

SHAKESPEARE: OTHELLO
John Wain

SHAKESPEARE: RICHARD II
N. Brooke

SHAKESPEARE: THE SONNETS
Peter Jones

SHAKESPEARE: THE TEMPEST
D. J. Palmer

SHAKESPEARE: TROILUS AND
CRESSIDA
Priscilla Martin

SHAKESPEARE: TWELFTH NIGHT
D. J. Palmer

SHAKESPEARE: THE WINTER'S
TALE
Kenneth Muir

MACMILLAN SHAKESPEARE VIDEO WORKSHOPS

DAVID WHITWORTH

Three unique book and video packages, each examining a particular aspect of Shakespeare's work; tragedy, comedy and the Roman plays. Designed for all students of Shakespeare, each package assumes no previous knowledge of the plays and can serve as a useful introduction to Shakespeare for 'O' and 'A' level candidates as well as for students at colleges and institutes of further, higher and adult education.

The material is based on the New Shakespeare Company Workshops at the Roundhouse, adapted and extended for television. By combining the resources of television and a small theatre company, this exploration of Shakespeare's plays offers insights into varied interpretations, presentation, styles of acting as well as useful background information.

While being no substitute for seeing the whole plays in performance, it is envisaged that these video cassettes will impart something of the original excitement of the theatrical experience, and serve as a welcome complement to textual analysis leading to an enriched and broader view of the plays.

Each package consists of:

* the Macmillan Shakespeare editions of the plays concerned;

* a video cassette available in VHS or Beta;

* a leaflet of teacher's notes.

THE TORTURED MIND
looks at the four tragedies Hamlet, Othello, Macbeth and King Lear.

THE COMIC SPIRIT
examines the comedies Much Ado About Nothing, Twelfth Night, A Midsummer Night's Dream, and As You Like It.

THE ROMAN PLAYS
Features Julius Caesar, Antony and Cleopatra and Coriolanus

THE MACMILLAN SHAKESPEARE

General Editor: PETER HOLLINDALE
Advisory Editor: PHILIP BROCKBANK

The Macmillan Shakespeare features:
* clear and uncluttered texts with modernised punctuation and spelling wherever possible;
* full explanatory notes printed on the page facing the relevant text for ease of reference;
* stimulating introductions which concentrate on content, dramatic effect, character and imagery, rather than mere dates and sources.

Above all, The Macmillan Shakespeare treats each play as a work for the theatre which can also be enjoyed on the page.

CORIOLANUS
Editor: Tony Parr

THE WINTER'S TALE
Editor: Christopher Parry

MUCH ADO ABOUT NOTHING
Editor: Jan McKeith

RICHARD II
Editor: Richard Adams

RICHARD III
Editor: Richard Adams

HENRY IV, PART I
Editor: Peter Hollindale

HENRY IV, PART II
Editor: Tony Parr

HENRY V
Editor: Brian Phythian

AS YOU LIKE IT
Editor: Peter Hollindale

A MIDSUMMER NIGHT'S DREAM
Editor: Norman Sanders

THE MERCHANT OF VENICE
Editor: Christopher Parry

THE TAMING OF THE SHREW
Editor: Robin Hood

TWELFTH NIGHT
Editor: E. A. J. Honigmann

THE TEMPEST
Editor: A. C. Spearing

ROMEO AND JULIET
Editor: James Gibson

JULIUS CAESAR
Editor: D. R. Elloway

MACBETH
Editor: D. R. Elloway

HAMLET
Editor: Nigel Alexander

ANTONY AND CLEOPATRA
Editors: Jan McKeith and
Richard Adams

OTHELLO
Editors: Celia Hilton and R. T. Jones

KING LEAR
Editor: Philip Edwards